LEADING
from the
SANDBOX ™

Develop, Empower and
release high impact
ministry teams

T.J. ADDINGTON

Leading From The Sandbox: Develop, Empower and Release High Impact Ministry Teams

Copyright © 2008 by T.J. Addington and Sandbox Resources™

First published in 2008 by:
Sandbox Resources
2332 Hallmark Ave.
Oakdale, MN 55128
www.sandboxresources.com

Distributed by:
Next Step Resources
901 E. 78th Street
Bloomington, MN 55420
800-444-2665
www.nsresources.com

ISBN   978-0-9791405-1-8
        0-9791405-1-X

This book is dedicated to
Grant and Carol
and
Ken and Barb
with appreciation for
many years of friendship.
One could not have
better fellow pilgrims
or greater friends.
Thank You.

To my prayer team
who sustained our family
through some dark days.

And to each member
of ReachGlobal
and
national partners
who faithfully serve
across our world
building His church.
You are a joy to serve.

Table of Contents

INTRODUCTION

When you think of the word 'team' what comes to mind? When I have randomly asked that question, peoples' first thoughts are often pejorative. Not because people don't *want* to be part of a team. But because their *experience* on a team has so often been negative, unhappy or even brutal.

Still, people crave team but they long for a healthy team where they can take the hill with likeminded people who share the same missional passion, and who work synergistically together in collegial relationships with clear, visionary, empowering leadership. Many of us would give a lot to find that kind of team.

The fact that you have picked up this book is an indication that you know that team matters … in spite of the challenges, frustrations and opportunities that all of us face in leading and serving on teams. We know team matters. We just want better team!

We know that done well, team can help our ministries go to new levels of effectiveness compared to what any one of us can do by ourselves. Good teams are powerful ministry accelerators that result in synergies, collegial relationships, missional alignment and enhanced ministry results. In other words, the return on mission can be HUGE.

Having done ministry on my own, on teams that were teams in name only and on some massively dysfunctional teams, and finally on a healthy, collegial, missional and passionate team, I will never willingly go back to doing ministry by myself—or on an unhealthy team. I love doing ministry with a healthy team of missional, passionate, collegial, aligned and competent folks who are committed to a meaningful mission. I have the double blessing of serving on that kind of team and leading that kind of team.

This book is written out of a passion to help ministry teams in the church, in mission organizations—in all kinds of ministries—develop this kind of High Impact Team for the sake of Christ's Kingdom. And, to make our common ministries fun—a joy in the journey. In fact, few things make our work more satisfying and enjoyable than sharing it with others who want to take the hill with us, who cover our backs, and who share our passion.

Over the past 25 years I have served as a pastor, organizational and church consultant on governance and leadership, and as an organizational leader. I have been on good teams and bad teams, and been fortunate to lead some great teams. Today I lead a global organization that is made up of 500+ people, almost all whom are on a team. My goal as their leader is that all of these teams would be healthy, missional and effective. This book is written for my colleagues in ReachGlobal and for my colleagues who lead and serve on ministry teams in the church and in other ministries.

What sets this book apart from other books on team? Very simply, it is practical and written as a 'how to' manual on developing High Impact (HI) Teams. This book will help you:

- Lead from personal health
- Hire healthy team members
- Deal with unhealthy team members
- Lead with maximum clarity
- Determine your central ministry focus
- Keep everyone aligned around mission
- Develop annual ministry plans
- Lead with a mentor/coach mentality
- Help people going through leadership transitions
- Foster a culture of empowerment and accountability
- Use the sandbox as a leadership tool
- Define the culture of your organization
- Become more missional
- Focus your team on results rather than activity
- Overcome the five dysfunctions of ministry organizations
- Help people minister out of their sweet spot
- Demolish silos in your ministry

ABOUT THE SANDBOX

I 'lead from the sandbox' hence the title of this book. I think it would be fair to say that *everyone* in our far-flung organization knows about the sandbox and what it represents. The sandbox is a simple tool that brings maximum clarity to your team regarding what your organization is about; and it keeps the big rocks of mission, guiding values, central ministry focus and culture out in front at all times. Furthermore, it allows leaders to empower people within clearly defined boundaries and brings alignment, not around methodology, but around ministry philosophy. The sandbox is a leadership metaphor!

If you played in a sandbox as a youngster my guess is that you have pleasant memories. The sandbox was a place where creativity and fun were synonymous. But you quickly learned that the sandbox was only fun as long as two things were true: you got along with the others you were playing with and the sand stayed in the box (and not too many cats used the box for …).

I believe that our ministry should be fun, challenging and use the best of the God-given gifts and creativity He has given each of us. Like those early years when we actually had fun in our 'work,' the same should be true today. Leading a team is all about understanding the gifting of those we lead and then releasing them to 'play' to their strengths, literally to play in their work. But for this to work, the sand needs to stay in the box so there needs to be clearly defined boundaries we ask our people to stay within—and they need to play well with their fellow teammates.

The sandbox is about all of that and more. And it has a high 'get it' factor which for any of us who lead complex organizations or teams is a big plus. Chapters two, three and four unpack how you can lead from the sandbox.

HOW TO READ AND USE THIS BOOK

There are several ways you can read and use this book. You can read it sequentially from chapter one to nine. Or, if your organization already has a *clearly defined and functioning* 1) mission statement, 2) guiding principles, 3) central ministry focus and 4) culture (all of which are necessary for HI Teams to operate), you can start with chapters one and two, and then jump to chapters five through nine, which focus on building and leading healthy teams. If you have specific needs you want to explore around team, the title page of each chapter has the 'Clift notes' of that chapter so you can get a feel for its content.

If you peruse the book, read the title pages and pay attention to shaded portions (key principles). In addition, stop and read HI Practices and HI Moments.

Ultimately, my hope is that you will use this book *with your teams* so that together you can build the healthiest-possible HI Team. If you do so, the HI Moments and questions for individual or team discussion at the end of each chapter will be helpful for team dialogue.

If you resonate with what you read in this book, I encourage you to use it as a training module when you bring new members on to your team so that there is a common vocabulary and understanding about team. I also believe that boards will find this book helpful as they think about how they operate together or how their staff teams should work. My prior book, High Impact Church Boards[1] is specifically designed to help boards become healthier and more intentional, and church governance systems empowering rather than controlling.

---

[1] T.J. Addington, *High Impact Church Boards,* (Oakdale, MN: Sandbox Resources, 2007)

ACKNOWLEDGEMENTS

What I have learned about healthy and HI Teams has been a combination of my own mistakes along the way, observing great teams and some pretty bad teams, consulting with many leadership teams in the church and Christian organizations, and learning from others who did it right.

I want to thank Bill Hamel for the opportunity to serve on a great team along with Jot Turner, Steve Hudson, Alvin Sanders and Fritz Dale on the senior team of the EFCA. I owe a great debt of gratitude to each one who serves with me on the senior team of ReachGlobal (the international mission of the EFCA) that I lead. They are a dream team and I am blessed to have each of them. And to Lindsay who is one of the greatest team members one could have and whose support made it possible for me to write this book in the midst of a busy schedule.

My teammate, Steve Hudson is the guru of intentional living. Much of what I know and practice in this arena has been influenced by him. He taught our organization the concepts of Key Result Areas, Annual Ministry Plans, Personal Retreat Days and Annual Planning Retreats. In these areas I stand on his shoulders and am better for it.

I owe a debt of gratitude to the folks at ChangeEffect for their part in making this book possible, to Brian Kagan for his invaluable advice and to Pamela Hudson for her editing expertise. Thank you.

For 10 years, Grant and Carol have given our family a place to relax in the mountains of Montana. It was there that a substantial part of this book was written. Thank you friends.

T.J. Addington

CHAPTER ONE
The Fallacies and Practices of High Impact Teams

Many people have a faulty understanding of team. This includes thinking that team is about working with my buddies, getting my emotional needs met, perhaps doing life with my close friends, spending lots of time together, attending meetings or working on the same project. Or, that because we are a team, we lead by committee!

NO!

A High Impact Team is a group of missionally aligned and healthy individuals working strategically together under good leadership toward common objectives, with accountability for results.

HI Teams are different from most teams. They are:

- All about alignment of the whole organization around a passionately held common mission.
- Synergistic in harnessing the various gifts on the team and focus on the bottom line, which is delivering on the mission (i.e., achieving results).
- Egalitarian in culture where robust dialogue is encouraged.
- Led by healthy leaders who love to empower and release team members to do their thing.
- Characterized by a commitment to results, good emotional intelligence among members and meaningful meetings.

HI Teams do not just happen. They are developed and empowered to achieve ministry results.

There are many ideas of what 'team' means. The lack of clarity on the purpose, practices and relationships of teams creates tensions, frustrations and unmet expectations for many.

For the highly relational, there is a sense that a team should be made up of 'my best friends with whom I do life.' For the deeply missional, team is about mission and little else. Especially in ministry circles where relationships are highly valued, some expect their team to meet many of their emotional needs. Some love to spend time as a team while others would rather get on with issues that are pressing in their schedules and priorities.

There is also a great deal of angst regarding teams. Many of us have served on teams that were highly dysfunctional—coloring our desire (or lack of it) to serve on another team. Often, teams are teams in name only and, if anything, hinder rather than help our work or organization. Leaders are often ill-equipped to lead teams and frustrate those who are obligated to show up for team meetings. Both in the secular and ministry world there is a fair amount of cynicism regarding 'team.'

Differing expectations of team come from what we may have read about teams (much of it not very helpful), our own experience with teams (good or bad), and our personal make up. While there are many different kinds of teams, the thesis of this book is that High Impact Teams function in a way that maximizes their missional impact. In other words, High Impact Teams look different than the average team. My assumption is that you are reading this book because you are not satisfied with the often ineffective, average or low impact teams you have observed or perhaps been a part of. Or, you want to take a good team to the next level. In this chapter, we will examine the fallacies and practices of High Impact Teams.

FALLACIES: WHAT TEAM IS NOT!

Teams are not about working with your best friends

You may work with those whom you consider good friends but ultimately teams are about common mission, not surrounding yourself with friends. Missional friendships are different than personal friendships. Missional friendships are collegial relationships centered around the common mission you have as a team and organization. Personal friendships are based on common interests and passions, many of which have nothing to do with the work you do.

This does not mean that healthy teams are not friendly. In fact, they should be collegial. Members should care deeply about one another and may even share a fair amount of their lives with each another. However, the depth of friendships on teams will vary widely since personal friendships are based on shared interests and passions, while team relationships are centered on missional alignment. The important issue is not to confuse the role of 'team mates' with that of 'best friends.' The latter is a bonus but not a given.

The primary function of team is not to meet one's social and emotional needs

A good friend of mine whom I hired a decade ago to serve as the director of a ministry I had started confided to me his excitement when he came to our organization that "we would do life together." The reality was that as he gave more of his time to this ministry, I gave less of my time to it and ultimately handed it over completely. While he is satisfied with his role and has built his own team, he was initially disappointed that 'we' did not remain 'we' as the ministry grew.

All of us have social and emotional needs that must be met. The deepest of these will be met with family and friends. Some may be met by those we serve with but it is not a given. Our role on a team is a 'functional' one designed to achieve a specific mission. We may or may not be with our team long term. The team may change. Our responsibilities may change. Teams are not designed to meet our primary social and emotional needs and if we try to make them do so we will be disappointed when our needs are not met or when roles change.

When individuals see team as primarily about friendship it makes it difficult for them to be honest with co-workers about issues that need to be addressed. We don't want candor to interfere with friendship.

I love working with the senior team I am on which was forged years ago. We have been through incredible times together, endured many great highs and more than a few low lows. We know each other exceedingly well, protect each other, love to be with each other and are committed to one another. We have seen one another through individual challenges, have prayed for family situations, and have sharpened each other to become better people and leaders. I cannot imagine a better team.

But: each of us understands that we are ultimately together because of the mission we serve of *"Glorifying God by multiplying healthy churches among all people"* for the EFCA. Each of us has our own set of friends outside of work that meet our personal, social and emotional needs. Seldom do we socialize outside of work. We are deeply fortunate to work with people we love, respect, know, trust and value. However, we understand that our team is not built on our emotional or social needs but on the mission that we serve together. This is a critical distinction of a healthy team.

Team does not mean that we necessarily spend huge amounts of time together

Team does require time. More time than some who are consumed by their own priorities want to give. Less time than some who desire the comradeship and friendship of those with whom they work would like to receive.

If you joined a team when a ministry was small, chances are that you had a lot of quality time with one another. The pressures were not great, the staff was small, and water cooler time was relaxed. As ministries grow, however, time becomes more precious and the time spent with those on a team becomes more focused, strategic and missional. Those of you who are on a church ministry team and have gone from a small to a large church know exactly what I mean. And my guess is that the transition was painful because the nature of your relationships had to change as the ministry became larger and more missional.

Healthy, aligned, synergistic teams make adequate time for team. But that time is spent primarily on mission and secondarily on relationships. Remember, our primary and most enduring friendships are usually outside of work. The *purpose* of team is missional—which will take time. For some, that time will be a sacrifice because they don't want to be pulled away from 'their stuff.' For others it will not be enough because they are looking for the team to satisfy more of their emotional and social needs.

Team is not primarily about meetings

One of the greatest fallacies about teams is that they are primarily about meetings. They are not. Yes, teams probably must meet on a regular or periodic basis. But team has far more to do with how we *think* about our working relationships, our alignment with others in the organization and the common mission to which we give our energies, than it has to do with formal meetings.

The senior team of the EFCA, for instance, meets one day each month. While it is a sacred day that none of us miss and where we hammer through strategic issues, everything I do the remainder of the month is also influenced by my commitment to that team. Whatever I do as the leader of ReachGlobal (the international mission of the EFCA and the team I lead) is always informed by my commitment to align with the rest of the organization, and by my obligation to not cause problems for others in the organization—which means that I must be aware of consequences to other departments in decisions I make. Service on the EFCA senior team means that I must think of the whole, not simply of the part that I oversee. What I do impacts others! There is no option for me to play the lone ranger or to lead my ministry in a vacuum.

Team is not primarily about meetings. It is about a mindset that always takes into account the whole organization, its best interests, its success and the inter-related ministries we each represent. This is a far cry from how many team members operate in ministry organizations where outside the 'team meeting' they make decisions within their own silo without taking into consideration the success of the whole. The latter perspective causes turf battles, conflicts and misunderstanding.

Team does not mean we are all working on the same project

Team means that we are committed to the same mission but not necessarily the same project. A church staff team made up of the directors of key ministries are not all working on the same ministry but are committed to the same mission which must be integrated across departmental lines. On the other hand, a youth ministry team may be more focused on a single ministry or project. There are different kinds of teams, many of which do not work on the same thing. This does not, however, diminish the importance of the team, as we will see later.

Team does not mean that we lead by committee

Teams are not 'leadership by committee,' which is a terrible way to lead. Good teams have good leaders. Good leaders practice collaborative decision making so there is common ownership and buy in. But, teams are not led by committee. Good leaders bring proposals to their teams, or ask others to do so for discussion, robust dialogue, tweaking and ultimate agreement. But someone must be the leader or coach of the team.

HI Moment:

What are your expectations of team and how have they been met or not met on the team(s) that you are on? Which of the fallacies of teams discussed above can you relate to?

HI Definition:

High Impact Ministry Team. A group of missionally aligned and healthy individuals working strategically together under good leadership toward common objectives with accountability for results.

CHARACTERISTICS OF HIGH IMPACT TEAMS

HI Teams are groups of individuals
who are committed to the same mission

A team is not a team simply because it is called a team. Healthy teams are based on a clear, definable, well-articulated, passionately held, common mission. In fact, if there is not passionate ownership of a common mission you cannot have a High Impact Team.

One of the key reasons teams do not function well is the absence of a clearly defined mission that all are committed to. Many churches and ministries do not have a clear mission. In the absence of clarity of mission, a team will find some other glue to hold it together but it will not be very effective because it does not have a central focus.

I once worked for a Christian organization that was made up of good people. We met monthly for the Executive Leadership Team of about 20 people. While we were a church organization, there was not a clearly articulated mission or focus. Thus, the function of this 'team' was to share what God was doing in our lives (which I didn't want to do since I had little in common with many of my 'team mates'), what was happening in our ministries (which was interesting but not compelling since little we did was integrated), and to pray together (general prayers about general things). I did not enjoy these meetings! This was not true team. There was no focus. We were not aligned.

Contrast that with the senior team I am currently on where we are deeply missional, where we do all we can to ensure alignment of ministries, where the topics we cover are the big rocks (big issues) that drive our missional agenda, where we know one another, are all pulling in the same direction, have competency in our areas and are passionate about our mission. The contrast between the two teams—and the missional results—could not be greater.

You may serve on a church team, a mission team, a senior team, a mid-level team or a volunteer team. But, the glue that holds you together if you want to see significant results of your work must be a well-articulated mission that you are passionate about. For an HI Team, mission is everything.

HI Moment:

Does your team have a well-articulated, clear, meaningful mission that each of you is passionate about? Do all members of your team buy into your stated mission? If not, it is critical that you develop a common mission as part of your study of this book. (If you need help doing this, see High Impact Church Boards, part two, which deals with intentional leadership around mission, vision, values and preferred future.)

HI Teams are committed to alignment around a common mission

A common dysfunction of ministries is the lack of alignment between various departments. It is not unusual in church staff meetings for members to spend time reporting the happenings of their respective ministries without any concrete alignment between them. They essentially operate in silos, doing their own thing, oblivious to what others are doing in their ministries and while all the parts may be 'good' they are also 'isolated' and not part of a whole. Staff members are focused only on their slice and are not interested in doing the hard work of ensuring alignment.

HI Teams reject that kind of silo mentality because it keeps the organization from being great and from maximizing its God-given potential. It takes more time and energy to be aligned than unaligned but the results of alignment around a common mission are a quantum leap from the outcomes that result from disparate, unaligned ministries. Good leaders and teams take the harder road because it yields greater ministry impact.

A characteristic of good leaders is that they insist on ministry alignment around common mission. In fact, the foundational reason that we develop team is to ensure this happens. If mission is everything, then alignment around mission by all related ministries is a non-negotiable. Good leaders and good teams refuse to allow silos to exist.

HI Teams commit to common values, practices and commitments of the organization at large

Integration means that all members are committed to a set of common factors. In the mission organization that I lead (ReachGlobal), we have a common mission, a set of 10 guiding principles, a central ministry focus and a defined culture. No one gets into leadership in the organization today without complete buy-in with these four areas. In fact, a person cannot join the organization in a ministry position without agreement in these four areas.

One of the reasons that many teams and organizations are not more effective is that they are not on the same page regarding the big rocks of the ministry. For instance, the central ministry focus of the ministry I lead is to "Develop, Empower and Release" healthy ReachGlobal personnel and healthy national leaders. This is what we must do day in and day out if we are going to have the greatest global impact. That means that every ministry team within the mission must demonstrate that they are practicing this central ministry focus. It is not optional.

We have 10 guiding principles that influence everything we do globally. While we give personnel huge freedom to figure out how to do what they do, there is no latitude in their obligation to live within the framework of our guiding principles. Healthy teams commit to common ownership of the organizational values, practices and commitments.

HI Teams believe in the complimentary use of gifts

Why bother with team? A central reason to care about team is that healthy teams get far more done in a more creative and synergistic manner than any one person could ever do alone. I am fascinated that God designed the senior leadership of the church (elders, overseers) as teams and not as a single individual. When the early church sent missionaries, they sent a team (Acts 13). When the early church designed a ministry to take care of the widows and the poor (deacons), it created a team. This is a recognition that God gives various gifts to different people and when they work in concert with one another, the team is at its strongest.

Good teams are not simply a group of people indiscriminately thrown together for the sake of 'team.' They are carefully made up of people with differing gifts that, when combined, creates something far more powerful than any one of the individuals could accomplish on their own.

The senior team I sit on has six individuals. Bill, the president, is one of the most relational individuals I have ever met and uses the God-given ability to choose great team members and bring people across the denomination together. He is also a 'maximizer'[2] who always looks for ways to leverage ministry impact.

Then there is Steve who is the ultimate process person. He is the most intentional person I know, a great mentor/coach to others and has the ability to shepherd any process toward its intended conclusion. Fritz combines strong relational abilities with the ability to build team and cast vision for the ministries he oversees. He brings a deep passion for spiritual dependence to the team we serve on together, and the team he leads.

Jot is the one who has the great administrative gifts and who oversees finances, business and legal matters. Alvin combines strong strategic gifts with a passion to bring biblical diversity to our organization. I am described as one who can envision the future, cast vision and communicate effectively (which is why I am the writer for the group).

Separately, we all have strong competencies that by themselves are significant. However, when combined, the strengths of all six members create a powerful entity—an HI Team where our various gifts complement each other and create something exponentially greater than the sum of our gifts. This has a compounding effect on the end product of our leadership. It is a powerful combination.

Our commitment to team goes beyond our representation of the various ministries we individually lead. We do not come to the team as representatives of our turf, but rather as leaders who think of the whole. That is a critical distinction. While my primary job is to lead the international work of the EFCA, when I come to the senior leadership table, I am there to lead the whole, not the part for which I am directly responsible.

---

[2] Rath, Tom, StrengthsFinder 2.0: _A New and Updated Edition of the Online Test from Gallup's Now, Discover your Strengths,_ Gallup Press, 2007, ISBN: 15962015X

This distinction also requires my willingness to put my gifts in play whether it involves the international ministry or some other part of the organization. When we are looking at organizational issues, each of us willingly takes on responsibilities that are not directly 'ours' in terms of our day–to–day responsibilities, but that will help drive the agenda of the ministry at large.

On HI Teams, members are not there to 'protect' their slice of the pie. They are members of a team that is missionally driven and they are willing to do whatever it takes to help the organization as a whole accomplish its mission. This is the opposite of a siloed, protectionist, turf-driven mentality that infects so many ministries.

HI Teams think strategically and are execution oriented

HI Team members focus on developing the best-possible strategies for the organization at large so that its mission is fulfilled. While there is an important element of simple communication and coordination in team meetings (so the right hand knows what the left hand is doing), the real work of teams is that of strategizing together on the best way to move the organization (or their part of the organization) forward. Team meetings should thus have a significant portion of time devoted to current problems that need solving, opportunities that can be leveraged, and planning for the future. This is always done in the context of the mission, values, and preferred future of the organization.

While some organizations are high on planning, they are often short on execution—or getting things done. The bottom line for good teams is that they are results-oriented. Team leaders must ensure that discussion regularly comes to concrete proposals with accountability for who is responsible for doing what. These decisions are recorded in team minutes and form the basis for updates at the next meeting. If this one practice were followed on a regular basis, teams would be far more productive than they usually are. Too many teams find it hard to come to concrete decisions and are slippery on accountability.

*HI Team members allow others to speak
into their ministries, methods and results*

This is a logical extension of the descriptions we have given for HI Teams. Because it is all about mission! Because all that we do is in alignment. Because we believe in the complimentary use of gifts, and because we care more about the whole than we do our piece of the ministry, we are ready and willing to allow others to speak into our area of ministry involvement without being defensive or protective.

I remember when the current senior team I serve on decided to form a healthy team where we were truly interdependent on one another. Until that time I had operated like others in the organization, fairly independently. I was accountable to the president but not necessarily to colleagues. The freedom I had in my areas of responsibility was huge. Then we started talking about forming a senior, interdependent team around our mission, values and preferred future.

I knew what the others knew. If we were going to go from siloed to aligned, and from independent departments to one integrated ministry, I was going to need to submit to the team and they would have to do the same. Being a fairly strong leader with strong opinions and convictions, the thought of submitting my piece of the turf to the leadership group was tough. But it was absolutely the right thing to do, so I did it. And so did my colleagues.

Team means that we are willing to work synergistically with others and allow them to speak into our own areas of responsibility. There is a price to be paid if you truly desire an HI Team. But the payoff is far higher than the price. Besides, it is Biblical! None of us in ministry ought to be operating as lone rangers or without the humility to work with, listen to, and learn from others.

Many talk team but do not live team. And the strongest reason not to live team is the cost it incurs. It demands our time, a commitment to a common mission, commitment to one another and alignment with others, a release of our independence, a focus that is wider than our personal ministry, and a submission of our gifts for the good of the whole.

*HI Teams have healthy leaders who love to develop,
empower and release team members*

Healthy teams are not possible without a healthy leader who has enough self confidence to bring around him or her other highly competent individuals without being threatened by their strength.

A word to pastors here, of whom I have been one: we can be some of the most insecure folks in leadership because we are often unable to separate who we are from what we do. In the secular world it is not uncommon for staff members to have a serious work disagreement and to keep their disagreement confined to work. Opposing attorneys, for instance may battle it out in the courtroom and then go to the pub for a drink afterwards. They are able to separate the professional from the personal.

Because we are so wrapped up in what we do (ministry) and because this is our identity, we are easily offended or become defensive when someone takes issue with something related to ministry (we personalize it rather than take it as an opinion about how we might do something differently). Like many of you, I have been guilty of the same.

Healthy leaders are not defensive or threatened. They have developed an attitude of 'nothing to prove, nothing to lose.' They do not have the need to be right all the time, can separate who they are from what they do, and only want what is best for the ministry they lead. Thus there is no need to be defensive when someone criticizes or suggests alternative ways of getting things done. They are also willing to surround themselves with people who are better than they are in the area for which they are being hired as long as they are team players. After all, it is not about *us* but about the *mission*.

Healthy leaders are also empowering rather than controlling. The need to control or micro-manage others is a sign of a defensive or threatened leader—or one who incorrectly believes that if they don't control it, it will not be done correctly. If the latter is the case, we hired the wrong person. If the former is the case, we are threatened by the competence of others.

Good leaders hire good people, clearly define the boundaries of their work, and empower and release them to get the job done. They are also willing to give those who report to them honest and helpful feedback so that they can grow in their responsibilities. They realize that they will only maximize the impact of the ministry they lead as they empower and release good people, cheer them on and give them credit for what they do.

Healthy leaders are not autocratic but believe in and practice collegial, collaborative leadership. They allow robust dialogue and debate and help the group come to common conclusions and commitments. One of the reasons I have such great regard for my leader, Bill, is his ability to put together a strong team, allow that team to grapple with key directional issues, and then release us to get the job done. He is not jealous of his position or authority and we in turn don't want his job! I have worked for leaders who were threatened by other good leaders and it was not pretty. Bill understands what it means to be a great team leader and it is liberating.

For those of us who lead teams, there is no substitute for continuing to grow as healthy, effective, empowering leaders. Others love to work for leaders who have those characteristics and will be exceedingly loyal to them.

HI Teams are made up of individuals who are emotionally healthy

Beware of who you put on your team! Healthy individuals will make team work a joy. Unhealthy individuals will kill an otherwise good team.

Emotional Intelligence, often labeled EQ, is the ability to understand ourselves, know what drives us, accurately see how we are perceived by others, and know how we relate to others. EQ also measures whether we have the relational skill to work synergistically with others while being 'self defining' and allowing others to speak into our lives or work without defensiveness.

Signs of poor EQ include the inability to listen to others, personal defensiveness, unawareness of how we come across to others, lack of sensitivity to the feelings of others, inability to constructively deal with conflict, a need to control others, narcissism, and the need to have our own way.

Good EQ includes openness to the opinions of others, lack of defensiveness, awareness of who we are and how others perceive us, sensitivity to others, the ability to release others rather than control them, allow for constructive and robust dialogue, and the ability to abide by common decisions.

Healthy people make for healthy teams. Unhealthy people kill healthy teams. There is a growing awareness of the need to hire people who are competent, who have character and who fit the culture of our organizations. However we pay too little attention to the EQ of those we recruit to be members of our teams.

It is possible for someone to have great competence but to have low EQ and leave relational havoc in their wake. Don't put them on your team! In fact, if they cannot be helped to become healthy, they probably should not be an employee of your ministry because no matter how competent they are, the damage they cause relationally in and outside the organization is too high. The alternative is to put them in a spot where they will do the least damage to others.[3]

HI Teams are deliberately created

HI Teams are created to maximize the effectiveness of the team through the right set of gifting and needs in order to create the synergy, alignment, energy, wisdom and skills necessary to carry out the team's mandate.

When you consider adding people to a team you are building, you need to consider a number of questions:

- Does this person have good EQ?
- Can this person play at or above the level that the other members of this team play at?
- Do they have a skill(s) that will complement the team?
- Is this person a team player?
- Can they contribute to the whole rather than simply guard their turf?
- Do they fully embrace the mission and values of the organization?

---

[3] Two excellent articles on Emotional Intelligence are Leadership That Gets Results, Daniel Goleman, Harvard Business Review, March-April 2000, reprint number R00204 and What Makes a Leader, Daniel Goleman, Harvard Business Review, January 2004, Reprint number R0401H

- Do the other members of the team think they will fit well?

- Do they have the expertise needed for the ministry in which they will participate?

- Do they understand the implications of joining your team and the expectations for them as a member?

HI Best Practice:

When adding an individual to an existing team it is wise to allow the current team members to interview them and help the leader determine whether or not there is a good fit. Each time you add someone to an existing team the dynamics will change. Securing the buy in of existing members can help the process proceed more smoothly.

The higher the level at which the team operates, the more important it is to carefully vet new members. If you add someone to a high-level team who cannot contribute at the same level as the other team members, you have effectively reduced the corporate output of the team. The other members will notice the difference and it will become a demotivating factor. The same response would occur if you added a highly competent member who was unwilling to act as a full team member but operated as a lone ranger.

One way to ensure a good fit is to allow a potential new member to serve on the existing team on an invitation basis. That gives the team the opportunity to observe the potential contribution the new member might make without committing before he or she is ready.

Individuals should be invited to serve on a team at the invitation of the leader and the invitation should not guarantee permanent service on that team. For instance, take the senior leadership staff team of a church. Someone who plays effectively on that team at one period of a church's history may not serve as effectively as the church grows. The team leader must have the prerogative to add or subtract team members if that is best for the organization. If the organization outgrows the capacity of a team member or a team member becomes unengaged in the work of the team they should no longer serve on the team. Stating up front that team positions are not permanent lets members know that service on a particular team is not guaranteed forever.

Also, team service should not be tied exclusively to the positions of team members in the organization. The organization I lead currently has 10 members on its senior team, plus me as the leader. Some members of the team are there because they serve in senior positions of the organization. There are others, however, who are not on the senior team because their position demands it, but because their competence and capacity are such that I choose to have them at the table—it would be foolish for me not to have them at the table. Position alone should not determine who is on a specific team. Competence, capacity and what they bring to the team should also be considered.

HI Team meetings are carefully planned and executed

There are few things more irritating than to be required to attend meetings that are carelessly planned and poorly led. Leaders effectively set the tone for their team by the care they model in designing meaningful agendas, keeping the meeting on target and ensuring that the time is well spent. When this is not the case, the message to team members is that 'this is not that important,' and they will not take their part seriously. Too many leaders under-prepare for team meetings considering them a distraction from more important issues.

Team time is not an ancillary part of a leader's priorities. It is central. Team time is where leaders remind people of mission. It is where they plan, solve problems, dream, and whiteboard around the preferred future of the organization—or the slice of the organization represented by the team they lead. It is a time to pray together and tackle common issues. It is a time to learn together.

One of my goals in designing team meetings is that no one leaves without having learned something new. This goes for board meetings that I am responsible for as well. Another goal is that everyone present is reminded of the mission.

HI Team meetings encourage robust dialogue between members

One of the reasons team leaders must have a healthy EQ is that healthy teams encourage honest, frank dialogue about all issues with the exception of personal attacks. In our organization we constantly say we want no elephants in the room, and where they may exist, they need to be named and put on the table.

This does not work for insecure leaders who easily become defensive. Defensiveness is a killer of robust dialogue because it sends a clear message that 'this topic' is out of bounds. Topics which cannot be broached become the elephants that everyone knows are there but no one is willing to name. One can judge the relative health of a team by the number of elephants in the room—the number of topics that are instinctively known to be out of bounds.

The ability to have honest and frank dialogue without personal attack is a sign that trust has been established between members allowing them to evaluate one another's areas of responsibility without taking umbrage of one another. Team members will only develop this frankness when they see their leader encourage it and take an open, non-defensive posture.

Defensiveness is about 'us' while robust dialogue is about the mission. Ultimately we are about the mission so we need to put away our petty insecurities for the sake of the mission.

HI Definition:

Robust dialogue is the ability to freely discuss any issue of organizational or ministry importance with candor while refraining from personal attacks or driving hidden agendas in order to further the effectiveness and mission of the organization.

Because the ability to engage in robust dialogue is so critical it is important to understand what it is and what it is not. Robust dialogue is honest conversation about critical issues and it is dialogue, not attacks or pronouncements. Some people, in the *guise* of robust dialogue try to drive their agendas and it is clear from their questions and interactions that there is a critical and antagonistic spirit behind their comments. This is neither honest (the agenda is not stated up front and the attitude behind it is not healthy), nor is it dialogue (what they really want is their way), and does not fit our definition of open and honest conversation around missional issues.

Robust dialogue is not a 'free pass' to say anything we want to say in whatever spirit we want to say it. As Paul says in Ephesians 4, if our words are not constructive or edifying and our attitude one that wants the best for others we should not say it. Robust dialogue is always designed to help the organization be more effective in accomplishing its mission. It is never an excuse to drive personal agendas or speak without love and respect.

HI Moment for Team Discussion

- What are the critical elements of the definition of team and how do they reflect on how you do team?
- On which of the team characteristics would your team be strong and on which characteristics would it be weak?
- In your opinion, which of the team characteristics are hardest to carry out? Why?
- On a scale of one to 10 with 10 being the highest, how strong would you rate the team(s) you are on? Why?

CHAPTER TWO
The Power of Clarity

The single most important thing a leader does is to provide maximum clarity to those they lead about what is important to the organization and how the organization is going to accomplish its mission. Getting to clarity is the single most powerful accelerator to ministry results and organizational alignment.

The four areas where maximum clarity is critical are:

- **Mission:** What we are ultimately committed to accomplishing
- **Guiding Principles:** How we are committed to operating
- **Central Ministry Focus:** What we need to be doing day in and day out to accomplish our mission
- **Culture:** The ethos we need to have to accomplish the first three areas

The goal of maximum clarity is to empower your staff to make ministry decisions in alignment with your core convictions and, in the process, provide for a high level of accountability. Leaders clarify the important issues so that good people know how to proceed within the organization.

The 'sandbox' is a simple tool that allows for alignment around ministry philosophy rather than methods. The sandbox:

- Empowers good people
- Provides for maximum accountability
- Allows you to deal with staff who don't play ball
- Has a high 'get it' factor
- Helps you recruit and train people whose convictions are consistent with your own

The single most important thing a leader does is to provide maximum clarity to those they lead about what is important to the organization and how the organization is going to accomplish its mission. Lack of maximum clarity leaves personnel to their own devices to figure out what is important, and different individuals will come up with different answers leaving the organization without a focused, aligned ministry. General focus yields general results with general accountability and general effectiveness.

Think about this: Without maximum clarity, an organization will never have integration or alignment (around what?), will not attract the best people (they want to know what they are giving their lives to), will not know when they have achieved what they need to achieve (what results are we seeking?), and even leaders will not know how to intentionally lead their team (because they don't know how) or have a clear means of making key directional decisions (there is no grid).

It is not necessarily an easy task to achieve clarity but getting to clarity is the single most powerful accelerator to ministry results and organizational alignment. It is worth the time and effort it takes to get there. While a leader must take responsibility for helping the organization get to clarity, it is essential that the key stakeholders (boards and key leaders depending on the structure of the organization) take part in the process and are in complete agreement.

Without maximum clarity, you will not be an HI leader and you will not lead an HI Team. The sandbox described in this chapter is a tool for helping you develop the best clarity you can for the ministry you lead. With clarity, your leadership role becomes much easier because there is focus and common direction for you, your team and the entire organization. Maximum clarity changes the leadership and organizational equation in a huge way—for the good.

THE SANDBOX

In 2004, I was appointed Executive Director of a global mission organization that has over 500 individuals living in over 40 countries of the world. It was an organization with rich ministry history, had grown rapidly in the past several decades under my wonderful predecessor, and was focused around church planting (probably the single greatest unifying factor). However, there was little alignment through the organization as a whole, or even agreement as to what we needed clarity about.

Part of this lack of alignment was a result of the tremendous growth of the organization in the prior decades with the opening up of dozens of new fields and the growth of creative-access ministry in many places. I want to be clear that my comments here are not construed as criticism of the past leadership or mission paradigm. Times change, leadership needs change and I came into leadership at one of those junctures when a consolidation of gains needed to take place for the organization to be as effective and healthy as it could be in the future.

Being deeply committed to maximum empowerment as well as to clear accountability, the challenge I faced was how to clearly articulate the big rocks around which we needed to have agreement and alignment in order to release leaders and personnel to make their own strategic and ministry decisions at the lowest-level possible while ensuring that a global ministry remained aligned. The challenge was to bring maximum clarity in a way that resulted in empowerment *and* alignment through the whole organization.

Because of the lack of clarity, there had not been a high degree of empowerment in the organization. In the absence of clear boundaries as to what was acceptable or unacceptable, leaders regularly had to check with the international office to obtain approval for decisions they made. This is one of the many downsides of lack of clarity—people don't know the bottom line so they run the risk of making decisions that are not acceptable because the boundaries of what is acceptable are not clearly defined.

Over the first year I worked with senior staff and the board to bring maximum clarity to who we are, how we operate, what is important and the overall ministry philosophy that would determine everything we do. We focused on clarity in four areas that had to be defined if we were to truly empower our personnel while also maintaining accountability:

- Maximum clarity on our *mission*: what we ultimately were committed to accomplishing
- Maximum clarity on our *guiding principles:* how we were committed to operating
- Maximum clarity on our *central ministry focus:* what we needed to be doing day in and day out to accomplish our mission
- Maximum clarity on the *culture* of the organization: what would make it possible to accomplish the first three areas

Clarity on mission

The mission organization had been operating with a mission statement that was different from that of its parent organization, the EFCA. Thus, we brought the mission of the international ministries in line with that of the parent organization (alignment). Fortunately, the mission of the EFCA was very clear as to the end result of our ministry:

The mission of the EFCA is to glorify God by multiplying healthy churches among all people.

For the EFCA, the goal is to glorify God, multiply churches that are healthy and reach all people. The mission statement is clear and lays out the central issues: Church, multiplication, health and all people.

Clarity on guiding principles or values

Like many organizations, the mission had a set of values that were not even remembered by leaders or personnel and which did not always directly impact how ministry was carried out. The values, while good, were too general to be useful in providing guidance for how ministry was carried out. Values should be clarified in a way that actually provides significant guidance in how we do what we do. Hence, we chose to call them guiding principles to drive home the fact that these values were actually designed to guide everyone in the organization in how they make decisions and carry out ministry.

We defined 10 clear values or guiding principles that every leader and all personnel are expected to live by. As you read the following values or guiding principles, note that they actually describe how personnel will approach ministry. They are specific enough that it is possible for any leader to determine whether his or her reports are ministering in alignment with them.

ReachGlobal Guiding Principles
We are word based and spirit empowered

As a Word-based organization we are committed to ministry that aligns with God's Word. Spirit empowerment comes from intimacy with Christ, a deep commitment to prayer, watching where God is at work and always listening to His voice.

We are team led and team driven

Believing that there is strength in teams and in the voice of multiple leaders, we are committed to a paradigm of team leadership under a gifted leader at each level of ReachGlobal ministry.

We believe that ministry personnel are more productive when they are deployed in ministry teams and in community with one another. We will build strong teams with healthy relationships wherever we deploy personnel.

We are partnership driven

We are committed to carrying out the Great Commission in partnership with local churches in the United States, national partners and other evangelical organizations.

We recognize the Biblical value of healthy cooperation with national partners. This includes the avoidance of paternalistic attitudes and a willingness to appropriately share in ministry decisions that affect both parties. Healthy partnerships include mutual cooperation without either party losing its identity or ability to work toward its intended objectives.

We empower personnel

We are permission-granting—within agreed-upon parameters rather than permission-withholding. We help personnel discover their strengths and deploy them in ways that maximize their gifting and abilities.

We practice entrepreneurial thinking

In global ministry, one size does not fit all and, while our mission remains constant, the strategies to complete the mission vary and change. We always look for 'best practices' and better ways to fulfill our mission.

We measure effectiveness

ReachGlobal is committed to being accountable to EFCA churches and supporters for tangible ministry results. A commitment to effective ministry requires the accountability of measurements.

We do multiplication rather than addition

Understanding that the task of world evangelism is huge and that mission workers and resources are limited, we are committed to strategies of multiplication over addition. We are facilitators and ministry coaches who come alongside national leaders to empower and train them.

We are a learning organization

ReachGlobal is committed to providing ongoing training and equipping of personnel in life and ministry skills. ReachGlobal will only be as good as the leaders who provide leadership at each level. We will find, equip and deploy those who have the gifts of leadership and who have proven leadership effectiveness.

We resource for maximum ministry

A well-resourced organization is more likely to be an effective organization. It is the responsibility of all ReachGlobal personnel to participate in the three-fold resourcing of personnel, strategy and finances.

We are holistic and integrated in approach

Historically, missions have emphasized the Biblical mandate of ministering to the whole person in the name of Christ. This includes ministries of compassion, education and other ministry platforms in addition to those of evangelism and church planting. A distinctive of ReachGlobal is that all ministries are integrated into the goal of multiplying healthy churches.

Notice that each guiding principle is followed by a clear definition of its meaning. These definitions have been carefully crafted and edited over time to clarify as well as we can what we mean by the guiding principle and how it actually impacts how we do ministry.

Both the headings and the explanation of each principle are designed to provide maximum clarity. As you can imagine, not everyone in as large an organization as ours agreed with all of the guiding principles. However, leadership was absolutely committed to them and I spent the better part of 18 months meeting with staff clarifying these principles, answering questions and being the prime evangelist for them—something I continue to do.

Today there is no question in the minds of our personnel that we are committed to these guiding principles and that all of us are expected to live by them. These 10 guiding principles inform everything we do in the organization and influence how we do what we do.

HI Moment:

Does your organization have a clear set of values that are designed to actually guide personnel and ministries? Are they sufficiently clear that there is no question in anybody's mind as to what is expected?

(For additional information on developing values, see High Impact Church Boards, chapter six.)

Clarity on central ministry focus

The central ministry focus of an organization is the one thing that it must do day in and day out—the most important thing it does to help it fulfill its mission. The central ministry focus is the organization's most critical activity or perspective that has the greatest impact on missional success of the organization.

The question we had to ask was this: Given our mission of multiplying healthy churches among all people in a global environment, what was the most important thing we needed to focus on with a laser-like intensity to maximize our opportunity to fulfill that mission?

How one answers that question has huge implications for the effectiveness of one's ministry. One obvious answer for us would have been the traditional answer that our missionaries concentrate on directly planting churches. But how many churches can 500+ missionaries plant at any one time? Furthermore, one of our guiding principles is that we do multiplication rather than addition so this answer was not consistent with that principle.

Remember that the answer to this question ought to help your organization have the greatest impact on its mission and maximize its ministry opportunity. For our global mission organization, we recognized that we had one central focus with two applications: *The central ministry focus of ReachGlobal is to develop, empower and release healthy ReachGlobal personnel and to develop, empower and release healthy national leaders.*

It is our conviction that the key to our mission's effectiveness is having the best-possible trained and deployed personnel, and the key to multiplying healthy churches globally is to focus like a laser on developing, empowering and releasing healthy national leaders who in turn can multiply healthy churches in their environment far faster and more effectively than we ever could.

What this means on a practical basis is that everywhere we deploy personnel, the central ministry focus is to come alongside national leaders, determine with them what they most need to be successful in the multiplication of healthy churches in their context, and to serve them by meeting these needs. We are not there to do what healthy national leaders can do but rather to help and empower them to reach their own people.

The central ministry focus is the one thing that everyone in the organization must be committed to doing all the time. For many ministries this will be about equipping and releasing people into ministry. You need to ask, "What is the one thing that all of us must be committed to doing and that, if done consistently and well, will ensure that we maximize our ministry opportunity?"

A parenthesis for church leaders

The concept of focusing on developing, empowering and releasing others is one of the most central themes of the New Testament. This is what Christ did with the 12 disciples and it is what the leaders of the church were called to do by Paul in Ephesians 4. Paul says that the central focus of church leaders' ministries is *"to prepare God's people for works of service, so that the body of Christ may be built up, until we all reach unity in the faith and in the knowledge of the Son of God and become mature, attaining to the whole measure of the fullness of Christ." (Ephesians 4:12-13)*

The key to our ministry, according to Paul, is the developing, empowering and releasing of the whole body for ministry, rather than simply doing the ministry ourselves. Our ministry in large part is to release others into ministry. If the church saw this as its central ministry focus with its people, it would help us far more effectively fulfill the mission Christ left the church in the Great Commission.

Regardless of how one words it, the church's central ministry focus must be to develop, empower and release as many people as we can into active ministry. In verse 12, Paul indicates that people do not become mature unless they are actively using their gifts in meaningful ministry and he says that congregations are not mature until everyone is in the game.

One of the greatest dysfunctions of the church today is that of 'professional ministry' where we hire professionals to do ministry rather than to equip the Body of Christ to do ministry. I have no doubt that this is one of the reasons that in general local churches have so little impact on their communities and why there is so little difference between how Christians and non-Christians actually live their lives.

If every congregation lived out Ephesians 4:12 in developing, empowering and releasing people into active, life-changing ministry in accordance with how God had gifted them the local church would be the revolutionary force God designed it to be. There are churches that live this out, but way too few.

Clarity on the organization's culture

ReachGlobal now had clarity on its mission, its guiding principles and its central focus. The final question was what kind of culture we needed to have to deliver on the first three.

Why is culture so important? It is important because if you get this wrong, you negate your efforts in the first three areas. For instance, with a world population of 6.5 billion, and an unreached population of around 6 billion, it would seem reasonable that a mission organization would focus on deploying as many missionaries as possible to maximize its ministry opportunity.

However, a mission's culture that defines success as the number of missionaries it has may in fact hurt itself. Why? Because if many of the missionaries are unhealthy or dysfunctional there is no way the organization will be healthy, will be able to train healthy national workers, deploy healthy teams or end up with healthy churches. The culture one commits to has consequences—good or bad.

For ReachGlobal, the defining culture had to be 'health' if we were to get to the multiplication of healthy churches or develop, empower and release healthy national workers (note that health was a key word in both the mission and the central focus).

ReachGlobal is committed to establishing a culture of health: healthy personnel, working on healthy teams, training healthy leaders to multiply healthy churches.

This means that ReachGlobal had to define a healthy missionary, a healthy team, a healthy leader and a healthy church. It also meant that recruiting, assessment, training and evaluation had to include a significant component measuring health. Without a culture of health we would not be able to achieve our mission on an ongoing basis.

Once we had defined the culture we desired as a ministry, we then formatted all of our recruiting, team building, training, leadership development and church health materials to fit that defined culture. We had to infuse the culture of health throughout the organization.

In relation to this, the next chapter focuses on the culture of organizations, and in chapter four, you will have an opportunity to define the culture of your sandbox.

THE REACH GLOBAL SANDBOX

Remember that the goal of maximum clarity is to empower your staff to make ministry decisions in alignment with your core convictions and in the process, provide for a high level of accountability: Maximum empowerment, maximum alignment and maximum accountability!

Almost all of us can remember a time when we were young and played in a sandbox. The sandbox was a place where you could build whatever you wanted, let your imagination go, and whether you were making castles or roads with Barbies or GI Joes, it was a great place to be.

But there is one thing about sandboxes: they needed to have sides because if one of the sides came off, the sand disappeared and the game was over. As long as the sand was inside the sandbox, life was fun.

In ReachGlobal, we want our staff to have great satisfaction in ministry and be free to use their wiring and gifts to maximum effect while we make the greatest impact for Christ through the multiplication of healthy churches. We want our teams to be empowered, aligned and accountable. So we took the mission, the guiding principles, the central focus and the culture and we made them the four sides of the ReachGlobal Sandbox.

ReachGlobal Sandbox

We exist to glorify God by multiplying healthy chuches among all people

- Healthy personnel
- Healthy teams
- Healthy leaders
- Healthy churches

Culture of Health

Mission

Healthy Effective ReachGlobal Ministry

Guiding Principles

Central Ministry Focus

- Word based and Spirit empowered
- Team led and team driven
- Partnership driven
- Empowered personnel
- Entrepreneurial thinking
- Measure effectiveness
- Multiplication not addition
- Learning organization
- Resourced well
- Holistic and integrated in approach

To develop, empower and release healthy ReachGlobal personnel and healthy national leaders

What we then communicated to our personnel is that they have maximum freedom to "play inside the sandbox," to make ministry decisions consistent with the sandbox (empowerment), but that we would hold them accountable for staying inside the sandbox (alignment) and carrying out the mandate of the sandbox (accountability).

My central job as a leader in ReachGlobal is to provide maximum clarity to our organization as to who we are, how we do what we do, what we concentrate on, what our culture is and where we are going. All of it is contained in the sandbox paradigm. Everywhere I go, I unpack the principles, commitments and implications of the sandbox. *I lead from the sandbox.*

There is no question in the minds of anyone in ReachGlobal as to the commitment of its leaders to the four sides of the sandbox. For those who might question our commitment, my answer is "do not underestimate our resolve." This is who we are. This is what we are committed to. This is our central ministry focus. This is our mission. This is our culture. These are our guiding principles.

The sandbox provides maximum clarity

Leaders clarify the important issues so that good people know how to proceed within the organization. That is the central function of the sandbox. It clarifies. It defines. Interestingly, ReachGlobal had some personnel who did not want to live within the four sides of our sandbox and transitioned out. Our sandbox was not the sandbox they wanted to play in. In the absence of clarity, everyone can do 'what is right in their own eyes,' and while much of it may be good it is certainly not designed for maximum alignment, and therefore maximum ministry impact.

No one joins our organization today who is not completely in sync with the sandbox. It is the central description of who we are. It provides maximum clarity for leaders, recruits, staff, church partners and national partners.

Many leaders have not done the hard work of clarifying the core missional elements of their ministries. Values and mission statements are vague, a central ministry focus has not been identified and, while all ministries have a culture, it is usually not a culture that has been intentionally crafted.

Vagueness around key missional elements produces haphazard and often mediocre ministry because there is not a clear ministry focus or good alignment. Frankly, this is the key difference between ministries that could be classified as good or nice and those that could be called excellent and mission-driven. For instance, show me a flourishing church that has a significant track record and you will find leaders who are very clear on who they are, where they are going and what their culture is.

The discipline of defining your sandbox requires you to come to grips with mission, values, central ministry focus and the culture you desire to create. If you cannot define these four key missional elements for your ministry, and if everyone in leadership cannot articulate them and be in agreement with them, you are living with dangerous ambiguity rather than missional clarity.

The sandbox allows for alignment around ministry philosophy rather than methods

In the past 30 years, the world has gone from being black and white to color. In many ways it mirrors the transition from the pre-globalized world to the globalized world, and from the round world to the flat world. Many ministry organizations have not made the transition from black and white to color. I define the differences between black and white and color this way:

Black and White vs. Color Worlds

Black and White World	Color World
• One size fits all	• Multiple needs, multiple answers
• Few options	• Many options
• Uniformity	• Customization
• Command and control	• Empowered
• Top down	• Flat
• We are the experts	• There are many experts
• The world is big	• The world is small
• Uniformity around strategy	• Uniformity around values
• Jobs based on need	• Work based on gifting
• Information flows through hierarchy	• Information flows where needed

Do not underestimate the significance of the shift from the black and white world to the color world. We live in a different world than we did 30 years ago. However, many ministries have not recognized that the world has changed and they have not changed to meet the challenges of a color world.

Any organization that continues to act as if one size fits all, or where there is uniformity around strategy with a top-down leadership paradigm is destined to decline and face serious challenges recruiting good people because the most talented, motivated and gifted people want to live and minister in the color world.

Many missions organizations are facing serious issues in this regard. Some who have served long years resonate with the black and white world and resist change. Those coming in today are looking for organizations that live in the color world and the two cultures cannot co-exist. A mission agency must either transition from the black and white to color or face a slow slide into decline. The same can be said for many churches who have not grasped the changing landscape.

The core uniformity in today's world is around a common set of values, commitments, culture or philosophy. Methods will vary by context (different situations require different approaches). Empowerment means that people need to be able to make decisions based on the situation they face from any number of available options. If, however, there is maximum clarity on ministry philosophy as defined by your sandbox, ministry personnel can freely make decisions from any number of options or methods that are consistent with who you are to meet the needs they face.

Our organization used to insist on alignment around methodology but that is impossible in the 21st century. Today, we have more alignment than we have ever had and more diversity of methods as we work in 75 countries all with different needs. If you lead a church team, you know that the needs of different groups span a wide spectrum. With a well-defined sandbox, you can allow for freedom in methodology while staying aligned around the core issues.

HI Moment:

Does your ministry live more in the black and white world or in the color world? What factors do you see to support your conclusion? Discuss your views as a ministry team.

The sandbox empowers good people

HI leaders do not control those they lead. They clarify the boundaries that the organization is committed to and then release their people to find solutions that are consistent with those boundaries and therefore, aligned around the core issues of the organization.

Alignment is only possible, however, with maximum clarity. Once you have provided maximum clarity, you can release good people to find solutions that work in their context. This does not mean that you as the leader do not give input if needed. However, HI leaders clarify the boundaries and then recruit great people whom they can trust to lead in their area of ministry because they have provided the necessary alignment around the sandbox.

When leaders in my organization ask if they can do something, I rarely answer with a "Yes" or a "No." Rather, I ask if it is in alignment with the sandbox and then will probe (good leaders ask lots of questions) to help them get clarity around the wisdom of the option they are considering.

In large organizations like ours, the definitions and boundaries of our sandbox help mission practitioners in far-flung places of the globe to develop ministry plans that are consistent with ReachGlobal's commitments. Their supervisors encourage them to think through methodology that will work in their context and give them freedom and empowerment to make those decisions (with appropriate coaching and mentoring).

Whether your ministry is large or small, empowerment is only possible when there is great clarity and alignment around the core missional elements of the ministry. Once you have those in place, and there is understanding of what the implications are, good people can be empowered to get the ministry accomplished in alignment with your mission, values, central ministry focus and culture.

The sandbox provides for maximum accountability

Empowerment and accountability are two sides of the same coin. Empowerment is much easier with maximum clarity about what is important. Once you have maximum clarity, you also have objective ways to measure results. ReachGlobal can measure health results, adherence to the central ministry focus, alignment to the guiding principles and bottom-line multiplication of healthy churches.

Furthermore, the Key Result Areas (KRAs) of ministry teams and the Annual Ministry Plans (AMPs) (discussed in chapter seven) must both be in alignment with the sandbox and provide for ways to measure annual ministry results. In the absence of maximum clarity, it is difficult for personnel to know what they are going to be evaluated against or to hold them accountable. In ReachGlobal, all personnel know that their accountability is around their KRAs and AMPs and that these must be consistent with the sandbox.

The sandbox allows you to deal with staff who don't play ball

Because the sandbox specifically defines who you are, how you do ministry, what your central ministry focus is and what your culture is, it also allows you to identify and deal with those who choose not to live in alignment with your ministry. In the absence of such clarity, it is difficult to identify what you are unhappy about as a leader when there is an uncooperative team member. The sandbox solves that problem.

Lack of alignment by staff who refuse to play ball hurts your ministry significantly. They may be good people but they are hurting your organization with their lack of alignment. Their continued independence sends a powerful message to others that you are not serious about what you say you believe. Whether it is active or passive indifference, it is like the drag of an anchor on your ministry.

With the sandbox, ReachGlobal has an objective tool to address staff members who choose to step outside the sandbox and we deal with them on the basis that they are violating the commitments of the ministry. In the event that we are not able to help them live within the sandbox we help them move out of ReachGlobal. This is a recognition that HI Teams must be in alignment if they are going to be successful in what God has called them to do.

For us, this includes the culture side of the sandbox with our emphasis on health. When we have an unhealthy individual who is causing relational chaos or other difficulties on a team, we act in a redemptive way (and we are usually successful) to bring health to the individual, and subsequently, to the team. Where that is not possible, we will help the individual move out of ReachGlobal. To do otherwise is to hurt other team members and ultimately, the entire organization.

Many Christian organizations live with significant relational pain, conflict and lack of alignment when they are unable to deal with unhealthy or uncooperative staff members who hurt the team and work at cross purposes with the rest of the staff. In the absence of maximum clarity on the part of the organization it is difficult for even good leaders to hold these individuals accountable for their attitudes, behavior and ministry results.

People 'get it'

The sandbox is simple to understand, yet profound in its implications. Many organizations are either unclear about what they are about or so complicated that there is no clarity. If the average person in our ministry cannot simply and quickly articulate what we are about we have done them (and our ministry) a great disservice. Simplicity and clarity go hand in hand.

Most of our personnel have responded with enthusiasm to the four aspects of the sandbox. First, they appreciate the clarity. Good people want to know the boundaries and the big rocks of the organization. Second, they appreciate the empowerment and the freedom that empowerment gives them to use their creativity and gifts. Third, they like the fact that success has been defined and that they know the basis on which they will be evaluated. Fourth, and most importantly, they get it.

Not only has the sandbox brought clarity to our own personnel, it is also bringing understanding to the thousands of partners and church leaders who support or interact with ReachGlobal.

The sandbox paradigm takes a complex ministry (and most ministries are) and simplifies it to four sides that, when taken as a whole, quickly and easily explains the ministry.

The same can happen for entire congregations if leaders were to develop their own sandbox for the church and use this simple tool to communicate the big rocks of their ministry. In chapter 4, you will see examples of sandboxes from different types of organizations.

The sandbox does not say everything about a ministry. But it should clarify the core missional elements that make you who you are: your mission, your values or guiding principles, your central ministry focus and the culture that you are intentionally creating to support the other three.

The sandbox helps you recruit and train people whose convictions are consistent with your own

There is great pain in finding out that the wonderful person you recruited a few months or years ago does not really fit your culture or your ministry. Every time that happens, we ask ourselves, "How could we have avoided the error?" One of the ways to minimize your risk is to be incredibly defining on the front end as to who you are as a ministry.

For instance, if a mission candidate looks at ReachGlobal and thinks that they will have a career planting and pastoring churches by themselves, they will quickly realize that we are about equipping and releasing nationals to take on those leadership positions rather than doing them ourselves (our central ministry focus, side three of the sandbox). If their preferred situation is to minister by themselves, they will realize that we are about 'team' (one of our guiding principles) and our organization is not a good fit for them

The more clarity you have about who you are as a ministry and the more clearly you can articulate that clarity, the better chance you have of recruiting people who resonate with who you are. When it comes to training your people, the sandbox provides a simple and uncomplicated tool that allows everyone to hear the same thing.

BUILDING YOUR OWN SANDBOX

The sandbox has four sides: mission; guiding principles or values; central ministry focus; and the culture you are committed to creating. Start thinking about what your four sides would look like if you had a sandbox. Chapter 4 will guide you through the process of constructing a sandbox that fits your ministry.

HI Moment:

- In which areas does your ministry have maximum clarity and in which areas is there a lack of maximum clarity?

- What is the connection between the sandbox and the twin sides of the same coin, accountability and empowerment?

- If you were to take a stab at defining the central ministry focus of your ministry, what would it be?

- Where is your ministry living in the black and white world and where is it living in the color world? Do you see the need to re-evaluate practices of your ministry on the basis of this concept?

- Do the values of your ministry provide actual direction to staff and leadership and are they clearly known by all? Is there is a need to evaluate your values or how they are defined?

CHAPTER THREE
Defining Your Culture

Every organization has a unique culture that defines it. Culture is never neutral. Leaders must be acutely aware of the culture of their organization and intentionally architect the preferred culture.

Organizational culture is the unspoken ethos of a group of people including its beliefs, social behaviors, practices, attitudes, values and traditions—all of which contribute to a collective way of thinking and practice.

Culture has a direct impact not only on people but also on the ability of the organization to flex and meet rapidly changing opportunities and environments.

Many organizations suffer from one or more of the five dysfunctions of ministry organizations:

- Control
- Bureaucracy
- Mistrust
- Ambiguity
- Professional ministry

You do not need to settle for these dysfunctions or the culture you currently have but can proactively define the culture that you want to develop and systematically move in that direction. Changing your culture takes time and senior leadership must practice and be the champions of the preferred culture. Consistency of the senior leader's message over time becomes a key factor in creating a new culture within an organization.

Leaders who 'live the sandbox' demonstrate their deep resolve that the culture of the sandbox become the culture of the organization.

Every organization has a unique culture that defines it. If we have been in an organization for awhile, we don't even think about its culture—we have become part of it. However, it is worth thinking about because the culture will have an impact—positive or negative—on our ministry. Culture is never neutral. Leaders, especially, must be acutely aware of the culture of their organization. They must recognize that how they lead and do team, and what they put in their sandbox will impact the organization's culture.

HI Definition:

Organizational culture is the unspoken ethos of a group of people including its beliefs, social behaviors, practices, attitudes, values, and traditions—all of which contribute to a collective way of thinking and practice.

CULTURE MATTERS

As you ponder the definition above, recognize that culture is not neutral. Beliefs, social behaviors, practices, attitudes, values and traditions have impacts on who your organization is and how people act. They also impact the organization's ability to achieve its mission and attract and retain good people, and they have huge implications for issues like empowerment and accountability.

True Story

I recently received a call from a highly skilled, successful veteran missionary of 25 years who is seriously toying with the idea of leaving the full-time world of missions, getting a job to support himself in Asia and coaching church-planting efforts in his spare time.

For 24 years he worked for a well-known evangelical mission agency. He had great relationships there, but the agency was so traditional in its model that he concluded there wasn't a place for him anymore. He is convinced that missions today is primarily about coming alongside nationals and equipping them to plant indigenous churches—something they can do better than Westerners (he is right). The mission he worked for, however, is still operating in an old cultural model (black and white world) where it is the Western missionaries who plant the churches and supervise nationals. The culture of the mission he was working for was traditional, change-averse, unfriendly to new ideas and highly controlling, even though it has many good people.

One year ago he transferred to another well-known mission where he was to oversee church planting efforts in a creative-access country. What he found after visiting 15 of the church-planting teams is that there was not one that had a plan that could actually produce healthy church plants and again it was all dependent on Westerners. His comment to me was that the evangelical missions world in the United States is insulated, insular, uncreative, controlling, old school and he is questioning whether he should find another way to fulfill his passion to come alongside indigenous leaders to help them plant healthy churches.

What this individual was describing to me about these two organizations was their culture and, while he loves the people in the organizations, their culture (practices, beliefs, traditions, attitudes, values and social behaviors) was deeply discouraging and in his view, was counterproductive to what they were trying to accomplish.

As a long-time consultant to local churches, I have seen the gamut of healthy and unhealthy cultures. I have visited churches where the prevailing culture is critical and harsh, and others where there is grace and freedom. I have seen both controlling and empowering leaders, staffs who are in alignment and those that are siloed, cultures that develop, empower and release healthy people in ministry and cultures that do not.

A friend of mine is a consultant to para-church ministries in the United States. Several years ago he was asked to do an organizational audit of one of the best-known ministries in the nation. He interviewed all of the top ministry leaders and discovered that there was a great deal of unhappiness among them because of the controlling, dogmatic nature of the senior leader.

In his report to the leader, he told him that he was likely t. lose most of his top echelon of leaders over the next few years because of the leadership culture of the ministry. The leader laughed and said, "No one leaves this ministry." He was wrong. Over the next several years, each of the senior leaders left for opportunities where they could better use their gifts and abilities.

The bottom line is that culture matters. The best ministry people will not stay long term in cultures that are unhealthy because, like my friend above, they value as an asset the time they have to make a difference for the Kingdom, and they will not invest their lives where the culture does not support the desired returns.

Organizational culture has a direct impact not only on people, but also on the ability of the organization to flex and meet rapidly changing ministry opportunities and environments. Mission agencies that have a traditional, change-averse culture and are still planting churches one-by-one using Western missionaries as their primary church planting method are missing the mark. They could be seeing multiples of church-planting results if they concentrated on developing, empowering and releasing healthy national workers.[4] Their culture is preventing them from being effective in their work.

Church cultures that are controlling and do not empower and release good leaders and team members are compromising themselves missionally. Culture matters!

HI Moment:

Take 15 minutes and jot down one-word descriptors of the organization you are a part of—taking into account its beliefs, social behaviors, practices, attitudes, values and traditions. Then write a one-sentence description of its culture. When you are together with the rest of your team, share your definition of the culture.

---

[4] Exceptions to this concept are places where pioneer church planting is necessary because there are no believers yet or where missionaries are intentionally planting catalytic church plants to raise up church planters who are then sent out to plant churches themselves.

_____

_____

_____

_____

FIVE COMMON DYSFUNCTIONS
OF MINISTRY ORGANIZATIONS

As I have consulted with churches and ministry organizations, I have recognized five common dysfunctions that are part of many organizations' cultures causing a tremendous negative effect on the ministry.

The dysfunction of control

Control is the opposite of empowerment. Empowerment releases people within specified boundaries to use their gifts and abilities for maximum ministry impact with definable ministry outcomes. All too often, leaders or the organization's culture mitigate against empowerment and exercise stringent control over people and methodology.

Control is not always overt but it has the same consequences as if it were. My own organization used to insist that there were only a few ways to do church planting around the world. People who were entrepreneurial and tried other methodologies were sometimes marginalized because they did not use the prescribed methods. The 'system' (beliefs and practices) was the controlling factor. The missionary who called me yesterday was caught in the same bind. The very system of the organization prevented him from trying new methods or even getting a hearing on those methods although he had successfully demonstrated that they worked.

In local churches, many congregations have the sense that they must control their leaders, insisting that all decisions come back to them. Many leadership boards believe that they need to control the staff or they might do something unwise. Staff members often believe that they need to control volunteers to guard the quality of ministry, and on it goes.

The worst form of control comes in the form of a church 'boss' who has the power to hold informal veto power over any key ministry decision, and/or an insecure leader who must micro-manage staff and activities out of his or her need to know everything, have a hand in everything and take the credit for everything.

One of the strongest themes running through this book is that good leaders and good organizations and good teams empower people for ministry within appropriate boundaries and encourage them to play to their strengths in alignment with their gifts. Jesus empowered His disciples, and the leaders He left behind were told to empower and release others—the theme of Ephesians 4. Leaders determine whether their culture empowers its people or controls its people!

The dysfunction of bureaucracy

Bureaucracy is a first cousin to control because it is perpetuated through unnecessary 'toll booths' that must be stopped at and tolls paid before one can move forward. Bureaucracy is not usually created to control (although sometimes it is), but rather to ensure that right decisions are made and right directions pursued.

Boards that require all items to come to them before decisions are made, or leaders who demand the same from team members, or layers of organizational leadership and oversight often create unhealthy and unnecessary forms of bureaucracy.

In the absence of a sandbox-like mechanism to define the overall boundaries of KRAs and AMPs to give direction to individuals, it is not surprising that bureaucracy develops. It is used as a management mechanism (awkward as it is) to keep people and ministries on track.

I define bureaucracy as unnecessary toll booths that need to be negotiated by ministry personnel in order to move forward. Again, leaders have a significant role in whether or not bureaucracy is part of the culture.

The dysfunction of mistrust

Mistrust is often the child of control and bureaucracy. At its core, the dysfunction of control is based on not trusting others to make healthy and wise decisions. Control and mistrust are two sides of the same coin whereas empowerment is impossible without trust. If we cannot trust individuals or teams to make good decisions, we have either hired/retained the wrong people or we have not been defining enough on who we are and where we are going. Indeed, a high degree of organizational clarity is necessary if we are going to empower people or teams to make decisions that will be in alignment with the organization.

I am continually amazed by the cultures of mistrust that pervade ministry organizations. This mistrust hurts the organization, hurts productivity (people who don't trust one another don't work well together), contributes to silos (lack of synergy with others so we keep to ourselves) and ultimately detracts from our return on mission.

There is a growing recognition in the secular world that trust is a core issue that organizations who desire to be healthy must deal with. Patrick Lencioni sees mistrust as the central core issue of team dysfunction in his compelling book, *Overcoming the Five Dysfunctions of a Team*. Stephen Covey has written a significant book on organizational trust, *The Speed of Trust, The One Thing that Changes Everything*. Trust matters!

The truth is that trust ought to be most prevalent in Christian organizations where the culture of Christ should be more pervasive than the culture of our world. The culture of our world is one of mistrust while the culture of Christ is one of trust. This is an elephant that must be confronted if a ministry or team is going to be healthy.

PRACTICES THAT CONTRIBUTE TO A CULTURE OF MISTRUST

Approaching others from the outset with an attitude of mistrust

This is an attitude that says "I will not trust you until you prove to me that I can" (the reverse of how a healthy individual thinks).

An unfortunate and often pervasive attitude in the church and Christian organizations is a built-in mistrust of anyone who is in leadership. Rather than making the role of leaders a joy (Hebrews 13:17), it becomes a burden because leaders are constantly fighting against this damaging culture of mistrust.

Assuming poor motives

This attitude believes that "everyone is going to let us down or make decisions that we would not make." Unfortunately, many of us quickly default to a position of mistrust—assuming that the motives that lie behind the action or decision were bad. Invariably, when I have made that assumption about others I have found that when I clarified the situation there were no bad motives involved. There may have been poor judgment, or there may have been issues and circumstances I was not aware of, but the motives were not bad.

Believing something to be true
when one does not have the facts

Leaders often find out months or even years after making a decision that someone in the organization is deeply distrustful of them because they had assumed certain things when in fact those assumptions were not true.

Taking on someone else's offense

This happens when an individual takes on the offense of another person, usually without knowing all the facts. Healthy individuals understand that there is more than one side to a story and do not make assumptions without doing their due diligence.

Healthy individuals and teams practice three principles that directly contribute to a culture of trust:

- I will choose to trust you unless you give me a reason not to
- I will assume your motives are right even when I disagree with you
- I will be proactive in clarifying issues rather than assuming something to be true

TRUST BUILDERS: TRUST BUSTERS:

Choosing to trust *Starting from mistrust*

You can count on me to trust you unless you give me a reason not to do so. In the event that trust is broken, I will clarify how trust can be re-established. I will always start from a position of trust rather than a position of mistrust.

Being candid and up-front *Being vague and fuzzy*

You can count on me to tell you what I am thinking, what my expectations are, how I perceive your strengths and weaknesses and if there is a performance issue, what you need to do to solve it. You may not always agree with me but you can count on me to be clear about what I am thinking and why.

Keeping my promises **Breaking my promises**

I will commit to those things that I can commit to and you can count on me to follow through with my commitment. If for some reason I find myself unable to carry through on a promise, I will tell you. I will not commit to those things that I know I cannot deliver on.

Acting consistently *Acting inconsistently*

My life will match my words and you can count on me to be consistent in how I treat those who report to me, in the pattern of my life and in living out the commitments of the organization. Inconsistency will be an exception rather than the rule.

Listening carefully *Not engaging in real dialogue*

I will respectfully listen to and dialogue with you and will be candid in my responses. This means that there is always opportunity for dialogue, questions, clarification and my commitment is to carefully consider your opinions and suggestions even if in the end I choose a different path.

| *Being fair and equitable* | *Giving preferential treatment* |

You can expect me to act with your best interests in mind and to always seek to be fair and equitable in decisions that impact you.

| *Caring for people* | *Using people* |

You can expect me to genuinely care about you as a whole person and never simply use you for my or the organization's purpose. This means that I will also seek to engage you in your sweet spot where there is convergence between your gifts and our needs.

| *Self disclosing* | *Secretive or unable to 'read'* |

You can expect me to be appropriately self disclosing about who I am, what I am thinking, where I am going and my own challenges.

| *Empowering* | *Controlling* |

Where you are given responsibility I will empower you to carry it out within clearly articulated boundaries rather than micromanage you or control you.

| *Clarifying* | *Making assumptions* |

If it appears to me that you have violated my trust or acted inappropriately, I will ask you for clarification on what happened and why rather than assume that you deliberately chose to do something unwise or inappropriate.

Mistrust flourishes when there is not proper clarity, when boundaries are not defined (how do I know what I can and cannot do?), when communication is lacking (the more I know the more I can trust), when one must secure permission at many levels (why don't they let me make the decision?), or where healthy relationships have not been established with others (trust is dependent on relationships). Mistrust also flourishes when leaders don't live by the same standards and commitments that they ask their teams to live by.

Trust is an issue that needs to be constantly addressed by leaders with their teams. Many relationships in our world are based on mistrust rather than trust and we bring these biases into our ministries. Yet, in God's economy, there ought to be a huge degree of trust unless there is reason to think otherwise. Leaders either develop cultures of trust or mistrust.

I make it a point to monitor trust levels among my senior team. Where I think that there is slippage, I will find ways to address it because trust between team members is key to our success in working together. Members of healthy teams choose to trust one another and HI leaders ensure that trust is fostered by good communication, clear expectations and boundaries, elimination of unnecessary toll booths and accountability within clearly defined limits.

The dysfunction of ambiguity

Where there is not a high degree of clarity around who we are and where we are going, it is very difficult to know how to make good decisions (based on what?) or to know how to focus one's efforts. As we said in chapter two, one of the main jobs, if not the most important job, of a leader is to bring clarity to those he or she leads on what the organization is all about and the issues addressed by the sandbox. There will be no HI Team without absolute missional clarity.

Ambiguity is ubiquitous in ministry organizations. Often our mission is so broad that it cannot be quantified and our values so general that they cannot really be used to define who we are and how they impact the day-to-day activities of the ministry. Most ministries have never defined the central ministry focus that they must concentrate on day in and day out if they are going to have maximum impact. And it is rare to find a ministry that has thoughtfully and carefully defined the culture that they are committed to intentionally create for the health of the organization.

Ambiguity around these core issues makes it very difficult to achieve any kind of significant organizational alignment because one does not have anything with which to align. It also means that team members can claim to be in alignment whether or not they are because the alignment mechanism is so loose.

On the other hand, it is deeply refreshing to find organizations that are crystal clear about who they are, where they are going, the central ministry focus they must have, and the culture they are creating. Where you find this clarity, you also find highly motivated and focused team members who, because of the organizational clarity, have great personal clarity as well. Getting to clarity is hard work but it is some of the most important work that leaders will do and it has a huge impact on the organization's ability to see true results.

I have worked for the EFCA for 18 years in the national office. It is a great organization. However, for the first eight or so years that I worked there we had a very nebulous idea of what our mission was. We knew it revolved around churches and we were focused on the number of churches that we had. Apart from running good programs and focusing on church planting, however, it was very hard to define what we were about apart from being one of those 'denominational offices.'

About 10 years ago, a big transition took place for us as we worked through a process to define a new mission statement: "The EFCA exists to glorify God by multiplying healthy churches among all people." All of a sudden we had meaningful targets that were not simply about numbers. We are about multiplication of churches, the health of churches, becoming a movement of 'all people' in the United States, and reaching 'all people' globally. These four integrated foci began to drive everything we did.

At the same time, we determined that we had to be a service organization for the churches in our movement. We existed for them and not them for us! In other words, by helping our churches become all that they could be (the local church is God's chosen instrument to reach the world) we fulfilled our mandate. Our surveys show that about 98% of our pastors know and believe in the mission of the EFCA today. And, because our churches voluntarily give financial contributions to the national office, they vote on our effectiveness with their pocketbooks. In the past 10 years, the financial support of the EFCA National Ministry has gone up dramatically. All this is the result of moving from ambiguity to clarity and then living out that clarity.

The dysfunction of professional ministry

This dysfunction applies particularly to churches and mission organizations. It is the thinking that only those who are formally trained are really able to minister effectively. If you doubt that this is true in your denomination, just ask yourself how many pastors there are who have not gone through formal theological training and whether you can be ordained without it.

In the local church, this dysfunction shows itself in the areas where lay people are not given significant ministry responsibility and whether or not there is a concerted effort on the part of full-time personnel to develop, empower and release others into ministry. After all, the mandate of church leaders, according to Ephesians 4:12 is to equip, empower and release everyone into active ministry. Yet in many places of the world we have not done this, trusting 'real ministry' only to the hands of those who are formally trained.

Here is something to chew on. There is no intrinsic link between one's level of education and one's ministry effectiveness! Educators may want you to believe there is but there is not. I am amazed at people, for instance, who get a PhD in Organizational Leadership but who cannot lead anything. Because my work is international, I know hundreds of pastors who lead highly effective ministries who have never had formal theological education and often, have not even been educated beyond the secondary level (what does matter is that pastors have a level of education consistent with those in their congregation).

It's not that I am anti-education (I hold a Masters Degree in Divinity from a great seminary). What troubles me is the culture we have bred in our ministries that leaves highly qualified people out of the game because they lack a degree. In fact, when churches are looking for staff members today, the first place I suggest they look is inside the congregation for someone who has the appropriate skill set and who is spiritually mature. You know them, they know you and you know whether or not it will be a good match based on long experience—rather than hoping that someone you call from the outside will be a good match.

A special plea to pastors

If you are a pastor you have high expectations placed upon you to preach, be a great administrator and lead well. That you must lead is usually a non-negotiable. But, let's face it, many of us are not wired very significantly in the leadership area—and that's not what we signed up in ministry to do. Yet in most of our congregations there are highly skilled leaders from the business world who are just waiting to be tapped and their skills used in the ministry arena but they are left on the sidelines or asked to usher or serve in a role that is not in alignment with their significant leadership gifts.

God never asked us to be what we cannot be. All of us are wired and gifted in a few specific areas and everything else is a weakness. Our weaknesses will never be our strengths. We need to bring around us a team of qualified individuals who can play to strengths that we do not have so that we can play to strengths that we do have.

The most untapped resources in our churches are lay leaders who could use their leadership skills in the church, come alongside pastors who are not wired to lead, and as a team, bring a level of leadership to the congregation that would infuse it with huge energy, creativity and missional impact. When we don't tap into those resources we leave huge missional impact unused on the table.

What gets in the way of this happening? First, it is our assumption that as the pastor we must be *the* leader. Why? God gave different gifts and if that is not our primary gift we are fooling ourselves that He thinks we can be the prime mover. Certainly we must be a primary spokesperson for the vision but why would we expect that we must be the primary developers of mission, vision and strategy if that is not our gift? It is theologically contradictory.

Second, I think it is an ego issue. We look at great leaders who pastor large churches and we think we should be able to do that. Our ego gets in the way of realizing that their gifts are not our gifts. We forget that the mission and effectiveness of our congregation is more important than our ego and that we need help. Yet, surrounded by people who could help us, we refuse to share the leadership ministry of the church in any substantive way or to seek their counsel, advice or invite them to help us lead more effectively. One day God might ask us why.

Churches need good leadership. I am an advocate of finding the best-possible people and asking them to serve on the senior leadership board of the church and then to take the best of those leaders and bring them to the table to help craft the most missionally compelling ministry paradigm the church could possibly have. It is not about us—it is about Jesus and His Kingdom and bringing the maximum number of people to Him and deploying them in meaningful ministry so that we reach maturity in Christ (Ephesians 4).

The alternative to this kind of Biblical view of gifts and the humility to admit we need help is found in the ineffectiveness of so many churches today and in ministries that flounder. Bill is an example. He is the quintessential shepherd/pastor: high relational skills and great caring skills. His preaching skills were good enough that the church he led grew to about 500. Each time it reached the 500 level it was like it hit a ceiling, would level off for a while, then decrease.

The church was filled with highly trained professionals, many of whom had strong leadership gifts and several of whom led huge organizations. Over time, Bill invited many of these onto the board but once there, they experienced huge frustration because they were not invited to help lead the church in any strategic way. That was Bill's prerogative and he saw himself at their level and could not admit that he needed help (and these were his friends who desperately wanted to help him).

When a crisis developed over the lack of congregational direction and people started to migrate out of the church (lack of missional direction will do that), Bill clung to the belief that he was a leader and could solve the problem. He could not and eventually resigned, bitter and angry, under the pressure of a church in leadership crisis. Six months later he found himself another congregation to lead where the scenario played itself out again and two years later was asked to leave over failed leadership.

Bill and the two congregations could have been saved a whole lot of pain if he had admitted that missional and directional leadership were not his strong suits and had surrounded himself with willing leaders who would have played to their strengths while he played to his and together led their congregations to places of missional effectiveness. But his ego would not let him do this and the churches suffered because of it.

HI Best Practice:

Healthy pastors don't pretend to be something they are not. They learn to lead the best they can and surround themselves with other qualified leaders for the sake of the church's ministry and the Kingdom of God. Healthy pastors are not ego-driven in the leadership arena but missionally driven and desirous of bringing the best people to the table so that the church can be everything God wants it to be for His sake.

I think it would be fair to say that God wired me to lead. Yet I have a leadership team that includes ten other great leaders who complement me in areas where I often do not have strengths. Some of these people have formal theological education, some do not. All are leaders, all are mature Christ followers and without the team, ReachGlobal would not be what it is today or will be in the future. Most pastors will not have that kind of leadership capital on their senior staff team but they probably have that kind of leadership capital in their church who are waiting to be tapped to help lead.

HI Moment:

How much leadership capital have you left on the table because you have not tapped into leadership gifting within your congregation or organization?

BE PROACTIVE IN DEVELOPING A HEALTHY AND EFFECTIVE CULTURE IN YOUR ORGANIZATION

It should be obvious by now that culture cannot be ignored without significant cost. The development of a healthy culture is central to good leadership, a healthy organization and getting the missional results that one desires. The good news is that you do not need to settle for the culture you have but can proactively define the culture that you want to develop and systematically move in that direction.

Wanting to change the organization's culture is not about dishonoring the past but envisioning the future. Times, circumstances, opportunities and organizations change. None of these remains static. In fact, organizations that do remain static are headed for history themselves. We honor the past but we re-envision for the future—taking today's realities and opportunities into account.

Pastor Steven Goold pastors a large suburban church in New Hope, Minnesota. For most of its history it was defined by its white, upper-middle-class congregation and it has a long, rich history of effective ministry. Over the past decade, something dramatic happened. The surrounding community evolved into a multi-ethnic neighborhood of great diversity.

After much prayer, discussion and planning, Steve and his leaders embarked on a difficult, rewarding, risky venture. They were convinced that their church needed to reflect the neighborhood it was in even if it meant radical changes in its practices and culture. Rather than the culture reflecting its traditional upper-middle-class roots, they set out to transition the church's culture to embrace the less affluent, multi-ethnic nature of the community with a whole different set of needs and opportunities.

Think of the difference in culture between an upper-middle-class, predominantly-white ministry and that of a multi-ethnic, less-affluent ministry. The two are radically different. Such a transition needed to be deeply intentional and required huge resolve because, as you can imagine, not everyone was enamored with the need to change.

None of this transition dishonored the past. The past was honored and treasured. The rich history of Crystal Evangelical Free Church is the foundation upon which a new ministry and culture is being built as New Hope Church (the name reflecting the name of the community in which the church resides, New Hope, MN). But circumstances, ministry opportunities and a resolve to honor God in those new circumstances required a new culture to be intentionally crafted.

Steve and his leaders understand what many others do not—God gives ministries different opportunities in different seasons that require different responses. In the process, they set out on a journey of what I call cultural transformation which will impact everything they do.

HI Moment:

Take a few minutes and jot down some descriptors of the kind of culture you would like your organization to have. Then write a one-sentence definition of that culture. Remember that organizational culture is the unspoken ethos of a group of people including its beliefs, social behaviors, practices, attitudes, values and traditions—all of which contribute to a collective way of thinking and practice.

_____

_____

_____

_____

_____

If you think back to the sandbox of ReachGlobal you will realize that what the four sides describe is not only the ministry philosophy but also the culture that we are intentionally creating to meet the challenges of a new day.

As a mission that sent its first missionaries in 1887, Reach-Global operated very much in the black and white world in which it was started. One of my leadership challenges was to help the organization move into the color world with a whole different set of realities brought on by globalization and the incredible changes in our world that took place in the past four decades.

Like Crystal Evangelical Free Church, ReachGlobal was at a critical junction and needed to change in order to best meet the needs of a new reality—missions in a globalized world. So using the sandbox, we set out several years ago on what we assumed would be a five-to-seven-year process to change the culture of the mission, reflected in the name change to ReachGlobal—honoring the past but envisioning the future. Principles like teams, partnerships, empowerment and entrepreneurial spirit were significant changes to our culture, and ReachGlobal is one of many missions going through such transformation.

Changing culture has major ramifications. For ReachGlobal, it meant changes in how decisions were made (they were driven down to the lowest-possible level), how intentionally we lived (all personnel have KRAs and AMPs), how we do leadership (we have transitioned from a culture where leaders were ad-ministrators to a culture where leaders lead), how we work together (in teams, not as lone rangers), how we partner with nationals (we are there to serve them and their movements), how we view alignment (it is now around the sandbox, not around methodology) and how we view health (health impacts our organization at every level today: individuals, teams, lead-ers and churches).

The sandbox reflects the culture we believe ReachGlobal must have to be relevant in today's world, but this does not need to reflect negatively on the prior culture. At the same time, proactively changing our culture for today and the future impacts everything we do because culture is deeply ingrained in an organization and is the real driver of behavior, attitudes and practices. That is why it is so powerful, for good or for ill.

Ignoring the culture issues will inevitably put an organization on a slide toward decline. Using culture change as leverage to proactively lead the organization toward healthy and effective ministry in today's and tomorrow's environment can be a powerful accelerator for healthy and effective ministry.

Culture change or definition takes time

Culture is ingrained and it influences everything. Since most people naturally resist change, the gravitational pull back to the old norm will often be huge—and powerful. Beware of believing that true cultural change has taken place when superficial behavioral changes are made (people will do what they need to do even if they don't really believe in the change).

I am sure that there are a few in my own organization who are thinking to themselves, "We'll wait it out, and things will go back to where they were, like they always do." They are not bad people, just change-resistant people who like the old way (it is their culture). I am convinced that true cultural change takes five-to-ten years at the organizational level and is proven when the new thinking, attitudes and methodology become the norm rather than the exception. This is why pastors who are bringing spiritual renovation to their church face such stiff opposition. They are fighting the prevailing culture with its deep attitudinal and belief systems that influence and direct it.

If one is intent on significant cultural change it is often necessary to bring new blood (new leaders) into the organization who have not been part of the old culture and therefore find it easy to embrace the new. This will cause anxiety in the organization (as all change does) but these new leaders do not have to deal with the old baggage.

Be absolutely sure that your senior teams (in my case the president of the denomination and the ReachGlobal board along with the senior team that I lead) buy into the culture you are seeking to create. If you are a senior pastor, this means first your board. The reality is that the natural inertia of the organization will seek to bring you back to 'normal' so knowing that you will be supported at the highest level is key to successful cultural transformation. Their participation in the process is important because they will be your key supporters once you roll out the new cultural paradigm.

Your next challenge is the senior team you personally lead. Ultimately, every one of these senior team members must embrace the culture you are seeking to create or they need to be shifted or replaced. You will not know this immediately. Some people will give intellectual assent to a new model but they are actually incapable of embracing it at a deep level even if they want to. Some just won't get it. Some may not agree with it. But you cannot have senior staff members who sabotage it (directly or passively). It may take you 12-15 months to understand where people really stand if the change is great.

SENIOR LEADERS ARE THE CHAMPIONS OF THE CULTURE

We said in the prior chapter that the core job of the senior leader is to bring clarity to the organization about who they are, what their mission is, where they are going and how they are going to get there. While the senior leader does many other things, the reality is that if they do not do this, they have failed as leaders.

The sandbox is a powerful tool for helping people understand all of that—if it is carefully constructed. I can answer all of those questions with the four sides of the ReachGlobal sandbox and my first priority is to help the organization understand the sandbox and its implications. People may not even understand that what I am describing is a new culture, which is fine. What matters is that they start to understand, embrace and practice what the sandbox describes. The sandbox is my "This is the football" speech that I make everywhere I go. If I ever tire of being the evangelist for the sandbox and what it represents, it is time for me to turn the reins over to someone else because without a well-defined, clearly-articulated culture that the majority embraces, we will never be all that God has called us to be. And that is my goal.

This includes not only presentations but a huge amount of dialogue in groups, one on one, and by email (I answer every email I receive from our staff). It takes time for people to grasp the implications, deal with their anxiety and figure out what the new culture means for them. Helping them do this is part of the leader's job.

At times, when I receive significant pushback or skepticism I will answer, "Do not underestimate my resolve." I want our personnel to understand that this is not going away, that we will overcome whatever obstacles we need to overcome and that we are absolutely committed to living the implications of the sandbox. That knowledge, by the way, is very helpful for people who wonder if this is a fad or if leaders are really serious.

Consistency of the senior leader's message over time becomes a key factor in creating a new culture within an organization. Clarity and consistency over time are a powerful combination. What this means is that leaders themselves must be very clear about the organization's direction, believe it and be committed to it. Leaders who easily change direction engender skepticism rather than trust. Many people are more concerned with consistency and clarity than with the specifics of the direction.

LEADERS LIVE THE SANDBOX

I remember the day one of our leaders in ReachGlobal was talking to me about a couple on the field who were not healthy and really needed some help if they were going to be effective in the long term. I said, "Why don't you tell them that they cannot come back to the field until they have received help for the issue you are concerned about." "You mean I can do that?" he said. "Of course," I said. "It is the fourth side of the sandbox, healthy people." "Oh," he said. "I didn't know we could actually deal with it."

I had to smile inside. The reality is that when leaders always refer decisions back to the principles of the sandbox and insist that the culture being created reflect the sandbox, people start to get the idea that the organization is serious about the culture it has said it believes in. Routinely when people bounce ideas off of me and want to know my opinion, my response is, "How does it fit the sandbox?" Once they can articulate how it fits the sandbox, I am glad to have a conversation about the merits of the idea.

As a leader, I never want to violate the culture we are trying to create and I want to model what it means to live consistently with our commitments. One of our commitments is that we believe in teams and lead through teams. That means that I also lead through a team and do not make unilateral decisions on issues that should be vetted through my senior team. If I honor this commitment with them, they in turn will be likely to do the same with the teams they lead. My example and the example of senior leaders generally sends a strong message that we are serious about the culture we espouse and are willing to live out the implications of that culture.

Because our central ministry focus (the one thing we must do day in and day out, side three of the sandbox) is to develop, empower and release healthy ReachGlobal personnel and healthy national leaders, my time and energies must reflect that central ministry focus. Thus a major part of my time is spent equipping and training leaders within ReachGlobal and doing the same with movement leaders with whom ReachGlobal partners. The example I set in living out our core focus sends a powerful message to our leaders as to what we expect them to do as well.

One of our guiding principles is that we do multiplication rather than addition. This means that we are always looking for ways that 'multiply' the impact of ministry for the greatest Kingdom leverage (something every leader should insist on from their key players). The very writing of this book is an indication of my commitment to do multiplication rather than addition. What would happen if every key ministry player in every church and organization were required to train one or two others to do what they do as part of their job? All of a sudden, a church with a staff of five would actually have a staff of 10 or 15. That almost sounds like what Ephesians 4:12 is talking about!

Leaders who live the sandbox demonstrate that they have deep resolve that the culture of the sandbox become the culture of the organization. By insisting that all of their senior leaders live the sandbox, that demonstration starts to go deep and pretty soon it is evident to everyone that "this is our culture."

We indicated earlier that one of the five dysfunctions of the church is ambiguity. Ambiguity or lack of clarity about who we are, where we are going, what our culture is or what our central core focus is promotes a lack of organizational and cultural alignment. Do not underestimate the power of clarity and the ability to be very defining. That is the power of the sandbox when leaders live it and call their teams to live it as well.

USE YOUR SANDBOX TO DEFINE AND DRIVE CULTURE

It is liberating to realize that we can intentionally define the culture that we want to create for our ministries—whether it be para-church or the local church. You have already taken a stab at identifying the kind of culture your ministry has as well as the kind of culture you would like to have. In the next chapter, you will have opportunity to build that preferred culture into your own sandbox. In the meantime, keep thinking about your preferred culture and its ramifications for the values and guiding principles you adopt as well as the culture side of the sandbox.

HI Moment:

- Which of the Five Common Dysfunctions of Ministry Organizations does your organization suffer from?
- How did you define your current organizational culture?
- How did you define your preferred culture?
- How does your present culture either help or hinder the ministry of your organization?

CHAPTER FOUR
Building Your Sandbox

The sandbox helps you visualize and communicate the most important 'big rocks' of your organization and, in the process, defines the ministry philosophy and the culture you are intentionally creating.

The sandbox brings clarity, in a single picture, to the complexity of your organization. It reminds everyone, in one picture, of the four most-important rocks of your ministry.

The Mission side of your sandbox represents 'true north' and the reason for your existence. It clarifies what you want to accomplish.

The Guiding Principles side of your sandbox defines the core commitments you want everyone to live by, allows you to craft the kind of ministry culture you want to permeate your organization, and keeps your organization in 'safe waters' by clarifying those things that are non-negotiable.

The Central Ministry Focus side of your sandbox answers the question, "What is the most important thing we must do, day in and day out to fulfill our mission?"

The Culture side of your sandbox is the culture you are committed to intentionally create to maximize the impact of your organization.

The sandbox becomes your key clarifying tool for leaders, volunteers and members of your organization. The goal is for everyone to use their gifts and wiring in creative ways for the Kingdom of God but to stay inside the sandbox.

The sandbox helps you visualize and communicate in a simple format the most important 'big rocks' of your organization and in the process, defines the ministry philosophy and the culture you are intentionally creating. Because maximum clarity is the first issue every organization must define, the sandbox forces you to clarify mission, guiding principles, central ministry focus and culture. Without clarity on these issues an organization is doomed to mediocrity—something none of us desire.

The reason to define a sandbox is to simplify the complexities of your organization and provide clarity about who you are in one simple picture. Both ambiguous and complicated systems hurt otherwise-good organizations! If you cannot quickly, clearly and simply explain who you are, your own people will often not get it, to say nothing of those who are outside your ministry. The sandbox allows everyone to see at one glance, and to remember, what you are all about.

I cannot stress enough the importance of being able to visualize the key components of your ministry in one picture. If you are a leader, you may be able to keep the big rocks in your mind at all times. Most others cannot and will not. The sandbox reminds everyone with one picture, at one glance of the four most important rocks of the organization. There are no 'stashed away values' or lost mission statements or unclear cultural ideals. It is all there, in one picture, in a unified whole with the constant reminder that all four sides of the sandbox matter and that we are all responsible to play inside that particular sandbox. Remember, out of sight, out of mind—which is the reality in most organizations!

Before we look at 'real life' sandboxes, let's review the four sides and what they represent. Whether or not you choose to use the sandbox as a tool in your organization—you must come to clarity in these four areas to be successful in the long term. The exercise itself is critical.

THE MISSION SIDE OF THE SANDBOX

The mission of your organization represents 'true north' and the reason for your existence. Mission statements should be specific enough that they are clear but broad enough that they are rarely fulfilled. Mission statements do not define how an organization meets the mission but clarifies what the organization exists to accomplish. Here are examples of good mission statements.

The mission of the EFCA is to glorify God by multiplying healthy churches among all people.

The mission of Rockpoint church is to lead people into a life changing relationship with Jesus Christ.

The mission of Life International is to multiply life-giving ministries wherever abortion exists around the world.

Each of these statements presents a clear definition of why the organization exists and its purpose.

THE GUIDING PRINCIPLES
OR VALUES SIDE OF THE SANDBOX

I liken guiding principles to the channel markers that one encounters when piloting a boat in inland waterways. The green and red buoys that mark the channel are there for one reason: to keep you and your boat safe. They tell you that as long as you stay inside the channel, you are in safe water. If you choose to leave the marked channel, you are in unsafe water. It amazes me how many would-be pilots think they don't need to stay inside the channel and find out the hard way that shallow water or shoals are not good for their boat's hull!

In the same way, an organization's guiding principles are designed to delineate the safe water or channel that everyone is to stay within. If you review ReachGlobal's guiding principles (page 81), you will see that they delineate how we do what we do and provide concrete guidance to all personnel as to how they must approach their work. They are prescriptive in nature and measureable. Supervisors can dialogue with personnel on how well they are living by the guiding principles and hold them accountable if they choose to ignore them.

Many organizations have values that are so general they provide no real guidance and are ignored. I asked the president of an organization this week what the guiding principles or values of his organization were and he could not even remember them. Obviously they were of no help to him or others.

Guiding principles serve several key purposes that are central to a healthy organization. First, they allow you to define for all personnel the core commitments that you want everyone to live by. For instance, in our organization, 'team' is a non-negotiable commitment and our guiding principle makes it clear that all personnel work in a team context. It is a not an option and the guiding principle makes it clear.

Second, taken as a whole, guiding principles allow you to craft the kind of ministry culture that you want to permeate your organization. When all of your personnel are living by the same set of guiding principles, you start to get significant alignment.

Third, they keep your organization in 'safe waters' by clarifying those things that are non-negotiable. By doing so, you prevent the unintended consequences of traveling outside the channel markers into unsafe waters.

To get to clarity on guiding principles you can ask yourself these questions:

- What are the non-negotiables that apply to our whole organization?
- Around what things must we have absolute alignment by everyone on the team?
- What are the principles, that if followed, will keep our organization in safe waters?
- If we had to describe the most important principles of how we do what we do, what would they be?

To be meaningful, guiding principles are not merely a phrase or word but should include an explanation of what the word or phrase means in your organization. That way they can truly guide behavior.

A well-chosen set of guiding principles also gives your organization permission to choose certain courses of action. One of our guiding principles is that "We measure results." That sends a strong message to our personnel that we are committed to seeing measureable results in our ministry and that everyone in the organization must be productive vs. busy. What we measure is important, but the ability to measure is ensured by the guiding principle.

One of the guiding principles of a church I know is that "We are multigenerational." That means that they do not simply target one group of people to whom they minister (as some congregations legitimately do) but that they value and are committed to meeting the spiritual needs of all generations. On the one hand, this means that they *cannot* exclude people in our ministry decisions. On the other hand, it means that they *can* design special ministries to meet special needs. It guides and gives permission for ministry choices that we make.

Well-written guiding principles are not only the channel markers for the ministry but they empower personnel to make decisions that are consistent with the principles. They provide both empowerment and accountability.

THE CENTRAL MINISTRY FOCUS SIDE OF THE SANDBOX

This answers the question, what is the most important thing we must do, day in and day out to best fulfill our mission. If you cannot answer this question, you will not be as successful as you could be. It is not always an easy question to answer, but it is critical to define.

I believe the answer to this question for the church revolves around Ephesians 4 and the developing, empowering and re-leasing of people into meaningful ministry in line with their God-given gifting. Making that the central ministry focus in the church context would considerably change the equation for the impact of the local church.

For ReachGlobal, it is the developing, empowering and re-leasing of both our personnel and national leaders around the world. We multiply ourselves through others. For The Worship Network it is "Developing content for personal and corporate worship," since everything they do revolves around providing worship content in a variety of contexts.

The central ministry focus is not the only way to accomplish one's mission. It should be, however, the most effective and lev-eraged way to see maximum ministry results. In ReachGlobal, we could have our missionaries personally plant churches on a regular basis. That is a way to reach our mission. However, by focusing on the developing, empowering and releasing of healthy national leaders, we can see a quantum increase in the quality and quantity of healthy churches planted. If we stay true to our central ministry focus, we will see more ministry results than anything else we could do.

To get to the central ministry focus, ask yourself these questions:

- What is the single most important thing we could do on an ongoing basis that would give us the most leverage in accomplishing our mission?
- If there was one central practice that we need everyone in the organization to pay attention to, what would it be?
- If we wanted to see maximum ministry impact in line with our mission (multiplication rather than addition), the thing we must do on a regular basis is ... .

If you get the answer to these questions right, and if over a period of years you insist that everyone pay attention to and live the central ministry focus, your organization will start to see return on mission like it has never seen before.

THE CULTURE SIDE OF THE SANDBOX

The fourth side of the sandbox is the culture that you are committed to intentionally create to maximize the impact of your organization. For ReachGlobal, this has to do with a culture of health: Healthy personnel, teams, leaders and churches. The bottom line for us as a mission organization is that without individual and team health we will never accomplish the mission of the organization.

For the local church, I believe that this side of the sandbox has to do with a culture of spiritual vitality (however one chooses to describe that). Without spiritual vitality, there will be no fruit or ministry impact on the part of the congregation.

In High Impact Ministry Boards, I recommend that leaders define what a healthy or mature Christ follower looks like. That way, you are able to intentionally design your teaching to help people reach the goal of spiritual maturity in their own lives and thus corporate health as well. If you can identify those five-to-eight characteristics of a spiritually vital Christ-follower, this becomes the fourth side of the sandbox for the local church. As such, it also becomes the target that each ministry within the church pays close attention to so that all ministries of the church are helping individuals get to maturity.

One church has defined spiritually mature believers as those who:

- Understand grace
- Are growing spiritually
- Practice generosity (tithe)
- Are committed to Christian community
- Are using their spiritual gift(s)

For them, a culture of spiritual vitality would be defined by these five characteristics. They would use the sandbox to continually remind their people that these five areas of spiritual vitality are the goal for everyone in the congregation.

Examples of a local church sandbox

Bridgeport Bible Fellowship Church
Bridgeport, Connecticut

Love God, Love People.
We exist to share the love of Christ

We believe every believer should be committed to:

- Spiritual growth
- Worship
- Submission to Christ
- The mission of Christ
- The Word of God
- Fellowship and relationship with one another
- Community
- Service

Creativity
Humility
Resolve
Interdependence
Simplicity
Transformation

Sharing the love of Christ through outreach
and discipleship ministries.

Rockpoint Church
Lake Elmo, Minnesota

We exist to guide people into a life-changing
relationship with Jesus Christ

- Grace
- Growth
- Gifts
- Generosity
- Gathering

- Biblically based and Spirit empowered
- Humble dependence
- Gospel centered
- Grace filled
- Inclusive
- Community and world focused
- Leadership friendly

The central ministry focus of Rockpoint is to encourage
and facilitate everyone to actively use their abilities, skills
and spiritual gifts in service to Christ and the
advancement of His gospel (Ephesians 4:11-16)

ROCKPOINT CHURCH MINISTRY SANDBOX

Mission: (Sandbox side one)

We exist to guide people into a life-changing relationship with Jesus Christ.

Guiding Principles (Sandbox side two)

- Biblically based and Spirit empowered

  The Scriptures are the word of God and the guide for our lives. We neither add to nor detract from His Word in our teaching. The Spirit of God gives us the empowerment needed for living lives that are pleasing to God. It is the dual ministry of the Word and Spirit that gives us the ability to follow Jesus and bring spiritual transformation to our lives.

- Humble dependence

  We recognize that we can do nothing of lasting spiritual impact without the power of the Holy Spirit. Jesus said, "apart from me you can do nothing" of eternal significance, but if we remain in Him we will "bear much fruit" (John 15:5). We are therefore committed to humble dependence on God in each of our ministries through concerted prayer, staying close to Christ and recognizing that all we do is for Him.

- Gospel centered

  The heart of the gospel is that Jesus came to die for our sins, redeem us, transform us into His image, and give us eternal life. All of our ministries are designed to help people experience the joy of becoming one of God's children, experience the daily presence of Christ and follow Him more closely. We are committed to seeing authentic life transformation through the Holy Spirit who empowers us to live out the gospel in service to Christ rather than conformity to our world.

- Grace filled

  We are a community that practices the example of Jesus in showing grace to one another and to those who do not know Jesus. This includes forgiving one another when an offense has been committed, avoiding legalism in all of its forms, loving one another unconditionally and honoring individual choices in areas where Scripture is silent. We are committed to treating one another with love and respect and to follow the Biblical guidelines for conflict resolution.

- Inclusive

  All people matter to God and are of equal value in His sight. We welcome all who desire to find and follow Christ. We are committed to ministries that meet the needs of all generations and to go out of our way, like Jesus, to love and minister to those who are hurting, needy or marginalized by society.

- Community and world focused

  We have a deep commitment to bring the good news of Christ to our community and world through evangelism and ministries of compassion. We are committed to showing the love of Christ by meeting needs within our community. Rockpoint is outward looking in its focus and desires to be a voice of hope and help to those around us. Ministries of compassion are close to the heart of God and a priority for Rockpoint.

- Leadership friendly

  We believe that God designed the church to be led by a leadership board of Godly individuals who will ensure the spiritual health, ministry direction and intentionality of the staff and congregation. We are committed to strong leadership, working in team toward this end. We believe that healthy team ministry at all levels, working under the leadership board, will directly impact the effectiveness of our ministries.

Central Ministry Focus (Sandbox side three)

The central ministry focus of Rockpoint is to encourage and facilitate everyone to actively use their abilities, skills and spiritual gifts in service to Christ and the advancement of His gospel. (Ephesians 4:11-16)

Culture (Sandbox side four)

We are committed to a culture of spiritual vitality at Rockpoint Church. This means that our lives should be characterized by the following priorities that flow from the love of God and that define one who is following Christ closely.

- Grace

  God's grace in our lives is undeserved and cannot be earned. It is a free gift from a loving God who has redeemed us. We accept His grace with thanksgiving, live in His grace through the power of the Holy Spirit and share that grace with others through loving relationships, acts of service and the concern of Christ toward others.

- Growth

  The Christian life is one of ongoing growth into the character of Christ. We are committed to a culture that facilitates real life change rather than settling for a mere intellectual faith. We believe that keys to life change include the practice of prayer, time in the word and fellowship with others as well as a commitment to personal obedience to Christ.

- Gifts

  Our lives are incomplete unless we are actively using our gifts and talents to serve others and advance the cause of Christ. We strongly encourage every believer to be actively involved in ministry in line with their gifting on a regular basis in the church, and in our sphere of influence. We will only be fully healthy as a congregation when all are using their varied gifts which together complement and complete one another.

- Generosity

  Just as Christ freely gave his life for us, He calls us to generously share what God has entrusted to us for the advancement of His gospel. We take seriously the words of Jesus, "Where your treasure is, there your heart will be also." (Matthew 6:21) We are called to be a people who are stewards of God's resources who freely give back to Christ a portion of what He has given us and to care for the needs of others in the body.

- Gathering

The Scriptures tell us that we are to live in community with others within our church: To love one another, care for one another, carry one another's burdens and encourage one another. We were not designed to live in isolation but to grow, live and minister in a loving, caring community.

Example of an Organizational Sandbox

ReachGlobal Sandbox

We exist to glorify God by multiplying healthy chuches among all people

Mission

Culture of Health

Guiding Principles

Healthy Effective ReachGlobal Ministry

Central Ministry Focus

Healthy personnel
Healthy teams
Healthy leaders
Healthy churches

- Word based and Spirit empowered
- Team led and team driven
- Partnership driven
- Empowered personnel
- Entrepreneurial thinking
- Measure effectiveness
- Multiplication not addition
- Learning organization
- Resourced well
- Holistic and integrated in approach

To develop, empower and release healthy ReachGlobal personnel and healthy national leaders

HI Moment:

- Which of the four sides of the sandbox have you clarified in your ministry?
- Are there sides that you think you should clarify for the sake of your ministry?
- Do you think that building a sandbox for your ministry would help leaders, staff and constituents better understand what you are about? Discuss the perceptions of your team.
- Take a few minutes and try to identify what a sandbox for your organization would look like and then share your results with the team.

CHAPTER FIVE
Healthy Team Leaders

Teams will only be as good as the leaders who lead them.

Good leaders have made the transition from being an independent producer to leading through team. It is no longer about *me* but about *us*. They have made the shift from 'how I would do things' to empowering other good people to do things as they would do them—in line with their gifting and skills. They have transitioned from 'hands on' in the details to helping define the 'big rocks' and allowing others to take care of the details.

Healthy leaders intentionally take on a servant role and prioritize the health and results of the team, not the status or power of the leader. This allows them to hire or recruit people who are even better than themselves.

Healthy leaders pay attention to the five priorities of every leader:

1. Personal Development: Ensuring that they live an intentional life in their spiritual, emotional, relational and professional life.
2. Strategic Leadership: Providing strategic leadership to the organization or the part of the organization that they lead.
3. Strong Team: Building a healthy, unified, aligned, strategic and results-oriented team.
4. Leadership Development: Developing current and future leaders.
5. Mobilizing Resources: Mobilizing key resources necessary for the ministry of the team to flourish.

And, they manage their dark side.

Teams will only be as good as the leaders who lead them. And, good team leadership is usually learned so my word to leaders who are reading this chapter is this: don't be intimidated and don't judge yourself as you read. Look for those areas where you can grow as an HI Team leader. Remember, there are no perfect leaders, only good leaders who constantly grow their leadership quotient.

THE JOURNEY FROM INDEPENDENT PRODUCER TO LEADING THROUGH TEAM

Many pastors and Christian organizational leaders did not sign up for ministry to lead others. They heard the call of God, wanted to make a difference for His Kingdom and entered ministry. It was a shock for some to wake up one day and realize "I am a leader and I've got to lead a staff, and I don't really like doing it." As one pastor of a church of 800 put it to me, "T.J., I now have 10 staff members and I really don't like leading them. I love to preach but I don't like the job of leading staff and some of them are a real pain. Help!"

This pastor loved to do what he signed up to do: preach. He was good at it and found himself in a growing church with multiple staff. Now, in a large church with a large staff he sensed that the stakes were higher, that he needed to lead better but it was not what he knew how to do. It was not his 'sweet spot.' There are countless Christian leaders and pastors who feel the same way and face the same challenge.

I remember when I was an independent producer. I was a staff of one with an assistant. It was convenient: one person to oversee, my schedule was my own, I could focus on things I wanted to focus on and, while my work affected others, I was not personally responsible for them. Today, the picture is different. I have a staff of over 500 with 10 senior leaders who directly or indirectly report to me. What I do, how I spend my time, and what my priorities are all directly affect others—and my ability to lead them well. The transition from independent producer to the leader of a staff of various sizes was not without its bumps and its lessons because the two kinds of responsibilities are very different.

Life for an independent producer is fairly simple. Life for a leader who leads staff or a team is much more complex. A leader of others must make critical transitions in how they think and act. They must transition:

- From thinking about "how I drive ministry myself" to "how I drive ministry through other good people." It is no longer about me as much as it is about us.
- From "how I would do things" to "empowering other good people to do things as they would do them"—in line with their gifting and skills.
- From "I can do life as I like to arrange it" to "I need to take into account all those on my team and how I can best serve them and help them become the best they can be."
- From player to coach. The larger my staff (volunteer or paid), the more I must transition from player to coach. It is not possible for me to ignore my team. If I do, they go south on me attitudinally or we develop silos without alignment.
- From 'hands on' in the details to helping define the 'big rocks' and allowing others to take care of the details.
- From "I can determine the plan and strategy" to "we need to determine and own a common strategy."
- From "I have a meeting to go to" to "I have a meeting that I need to carefully prepare for and lead."
- From "my opinion is the one that counts" to "I need to be collaborative in my thinking, and decision making." And, "I need to encourage robust dialogue around issues and take a non-defensive posture when others disagree with me."

These are not easy transitions and there is significant leadership pain and even attrition when leaders go from being solo producers to team leaders and don't understand the need to do life differently. It is not uncommon for pastors who suddenly find themselves saddled with reports and a team who have not made the transitions above to face considerable unhappiness or conflict with staff. Often they are not aware of why the conflict is occurring.

A TRUE STORY

Jon is a gifted communicator, evangelist and has excellent re-lational skills. Based on those gifts, he was the first pastor of a wonderful church in a professional, upscale community which has a good number of executive and CEO-type retirees. The makeup of his church board reflects this executive mentality.

Jon is gregarious, impulsive, likes to do things himself, resists any kind of schedule and his gifting allowed him to get a lot done without much planning. Because he is an ef-fective communicator, those who come to the church love what he does from the pulpit along with his outgoing, highly relational style.

All of this worked well for Jon until the church hit 600 or so, when there was growing tension between Jon and his board and staff. From the board's perspective it was time to bring greater cohesion, planning and organization to what had been run like a 'mom and pop' shop. Besides, they had just moved into a new facility from a rented one and that in itself meant a need for bet-ter organization. They loved Jon dearly, which was in his favor, but they felt something had to change. To put it bluntly, Jon's leaders were people who were or had been highly disciplined executives and Jon was a 'fly by the seat of the pants' kind of guy which became irritating to his board members.

Staff relationships had fissures as well. They often did not know where Jon was or what he was doing (he did not tell them and did not keep a written schedule), and they did not feel like they were being coached in their jobs (they didn't even have job descriptions so they didn't know what the real expectations were). Because Jon spent little quality time with staff they felt alone and devalued. It did not go without notice that Jon spent more quality time with congregants than his own staff—which he was supposed to be leading.

Because Jon was a creative guy, he would often come up with a new idea at the last minute and staff were expected to re-spond. Meetings were about Jon talking to staff rather than team dialogue. He was such a great communicator (debater) that they felt they would lose the argument when they disagreed with him (and they had plenty of experience).

All of this came to a point where I was called in as a consultant for Jon, the board and staff. Without intervention, it could easily have led to increasing conflict and Jon's eventual leaving. After interviewing the board, staff and Jon, I shared with him some of the frustrations they were feeling and how he was being perceived. Jon's immediate reaction was "but this is who I am."

My response was that if he wanted to continue to grow the church, he needed to make critical transitions in his thought and practice—to go from an independent producer to a team leader. Otherwise he would become a barrier to the church moving forward and the conflict would grow. The other alternative would be for him to go back and start another church where he could be an independent producer and grow it to 500 or so and then pass it off to a leader who enjoyed leading a team.

Jon decided that he wanted to make the transition, difficult as it was and the leadership quietly hired an executive coach to help him do so. Several years later he is still there and life is calmer and more peaceful.

Jon's pain in the transition from independent producer to team leader is not unique and some don't survive the transition. It is a transition of values, roles, how one does life, how one sees and builds team, what one's priorities and schedule are, and how well one defines who the organization is and where it is going. Moses was one of those leaders who had to make such a transition—going from an independent operator to a team leader (the story is in Exodus 18).

We have recognized in ReachGlobal that careful coaching is required when we ask someone to become a leader who has been doing primarily hands-on ministry. The tendency is for them to want to continue the hands-on ministry and add to that the leadership piece. Yet, with each successive step into leadership, the cost is that we must leave something behind if we are going to be successful in the new role. If the journey from independent producer to leading through team is not negotiated, we will not be successful as leaders.

This means that when we ask someone to take on the leadership of others it is critical that we help them understand the transitions they must move through and then help them make those transitions. Too often, we leave people to their own devices assuming that they will figure it out, a strategy guaranteed to cause pain to the leader and the team.

What altitude are you flying at?

A way to think about this is to determine the altitude that one must fly at in their leadership role. As the leader of Reach-Global, my responsibility is to fly at the 40,000 foot level so that I can see the horizons from the best vantage point. My senior team members need to be at 30,000 feet and their area leaders at 20,000 feet and many others will be at ground level.

When I default to flying lower than I should be (by getting into issues that someone else should be dealing with), I am compromising my leadership because I have defaulted to old habits and old responsibilities. My job is not to deal with 20,000 foot issues but with 40,000 foot issues.

Joel is a leader who rose through the ranks of a mission organization to become a senior leader in that organization. He started as a missionary 'on the ground,' then became a team leader, soon an area leader and then a senior leader. In this role he needed to be flying at 30,000 feet but there were things he loved to do at the 5,000 foot level and he had a habit of 'losing altitude' to get into things he used to do and enjoyed doing. Yet he was now responsible for a huge area of the world, scores of missionaries and many national partnerships.

His leader had to coach him to stay at the 30,000 foot level. Could he still do the things he used to do? Not personally. If he wanted those projects to get done he had to find someone to do it *through* rather than doing it *himself.* His altitude was 30,000 feet as a leader, not 5,000 feet. It took coaching and practice but he learned to stay at the right altitude.

This does not mean that leaders are aloof or distant from those they lead. Leaders are always with those they lead. What it means is that we are doing those tasks that are appropriate for our current role and have given up those things that were appropriate for our past role. You cannot take on new responsibility—and do it well—without giving up old responsibility. Further, when we hang on to the old tasks we disempower those who should be responsible for those tasks. Remember, *healthy* leaders make the transition from independent producer to leading through others. This transition-related pain of loss is a natural result of agreeing to fly at a higher altitude than we previously did. We will discuss this more fully in the chapter on Dangerous Transitions.

When pastors like Jon or leaders like Joel micromanage staff, and continue to do what they used to do when their ministry was smaller, they are flying at the wrong altitude. Understand the altitude that you need to fly at and stay there. It is a transition from a lower to a higher altitude. It requires you to give things away, empower others and ultimately to lead at the level you need to lead at. When you lead at the right altitude, you allow others to lead at their appropriate altitude.

HI Moment:

If you are a leader of others, take a moment and reflect on your transition from independent producer to a leader of others. What were the tough spots for you?

HI Best Practice:

If you are a leader going through this kind of transition, find someone who has successfully navigated the change and ask them to coach you. Ask them what 'dumb tax' they paid (things that they would do differently in the future) and what personal and professional changes they needed to make. Having a coach through the process can save pain and make the transition smoother.

It is about influence and results, not status or power

To be a good team leader one must intentionally take on a servant role and prioritize the health and results of the team, not the status or power of the leader. Commitment to team means that we no longer take credit but give credit away for accomplishments to those on the team. We intentionally platform and hold up team members, allowing our influence to flow through them so they have the moral authority to do what they must do in the organization.

One of the tests of great leadership is whether a leader needs the spotlight, adulation, praise or credit for the results of the team's work. Great leaders point all of this toward the team because it was the team that accomplished the work. Insecure or narcissist leaders require that they be the center, essentially stealing credit from those who were actually responsible. And don't be fooled, people notice, especially the team who made it happen!

Power, status, spotlight and praise are a deadly aphrodisiac for unhealthy leaders who think it is all about them. They are often charismatic and visionary but they are seldom able to build a strong, unified, results-oriented team because ultimately, it is always about them. Eventually they implode, causing pain for those around them. Unfortunately too many of these addicts find their way into ministry: stay away from them. When it comes apart it is ugly.

Every organization has levels and lines of authority. In healthy teams, however, there is an egalitarian ethos where the leader is a coach and a cheerleader for the team—and all sit at the table as peers with the ability to make an equal contribution. After all, this is NOT about the leader. It is a about team that, when working together, can see results that are a quantum leap from what any one individual could produce. Leaders, like Jon, who dominate meetings don't get it and send the message that the team is about 'me' not 'us.'

In the end, the job of the team leader is to ensure the success of others, to empower them to do what they can do better than them, to be their coach and cheerleader, and to allow them to see the fruits of their work. When praise comes to the leader, it is wisdom to hold up others because they are responsible for the vast majority of good things that happen. Status and power are not important to good leaders: influence and results are. Good leaders give others the praise for successes and take personal responsibility for failures.

Healthy leaders build teams of people who are more competent than themselves in the roles they are hired for

Think about that for a moment! To be willing to do that takes a lot of personal security, a commitment to mission and a deep resolve to build the best team we can for the best ministry results we can get. Insecure leaders hire less-competent people than themselves because they are threatened by those who are strong in their own right. They want to have the final word and strong people, appropriately, will challenge the status quo.

This is one of the shifts in thinking that we need to make when we go from independent producer to leading through team. We will only be as good as our team. Our ministry success will reflect the quality of the team that runs it. Our role is like an orchestra director who ensures that great musicians are recruited—all great in their own right—and are playing from the same music score at the same tempo.

My own leader is a master at this and I have deep respect for him. He has assembled a great team, has empowered us, is not intimidated by us and allows us to play to our strengths. If you have served on a team with that kind of leader you know how wonderful it is.

As you build your team and you identify needed roles (which will be different from yours, otherwise they are redundant), look for the very best people you can find. Generally if they are not more qualified than you are in their role, you have the wrong person. You cannot give great guidance in an area that is not your strength. You can outline outcomes but they have to figure out strategy which is why they need to be great at what they do—and be better than you would be at that role.

I am not a great detail person so I hired the very best—Lindsay, who 'runs my life.' I can give her feedback on what success for her looks like, but if I had to tell her how to do what she needs to do—I would have hired the wrong person. She is better than I would be in her role, which is why I hired her.

It should be obvious by now that the Emotional Intelligence (EQ) of the team leader plays a major role in developing and maintaining healthy teams. The better we know ourselves and the healthier our EQ, the better leader we will be.

WHAT GOOD LEADERS DO

Good leaders must do at least five things well in their leadership role. There may be other things a leader does but if she or he does not do these five things well, they will not become great leaders. These five responsibilities are the five highest priorities *in one's leadership role.* How well they are done will determine the effectiveness of the team.

Pastors who read this may push back and say, "I do a lot of other things." That is true. But in your leadership role, these five responsibilities are critical. For each of these five priorities there should be an annual plan that a leader is committed to following.

One: Personal Development— Ensuring that I live intentionally in my spiritual, family, emotional, relational and professional life

By personal development I mean the core issues that make and keep a leader healthy spiritually, relationally, emotionally and professionally. These become a leader's highest priority because health in these areas determines their ability to lead spiritually and professionally and to model the kind of faithful, fruitful, connected life that the New Testament describes for leaders.

The six areas of personal development take into account:
- My marriage (if married)
- My children (if I have them)
- My relationship with Christ (keeping it vital)
- My understanding of myself and my wiring (EQ)
- My professional development
- My skill as a leader

These areas of development go to a core truth: healthy leaders are those who pay close attention to their own lives so that they can lead out of spiritual, emotional and relational health.

As the Apostle Paul wrote to Timothy, "Watch your life and doctrine closely." (1 Timothy 4:16)

The higher the level of leadership one has, the greater the temptation to take short cuts in personal development because the leadership demands become so heavy. Those who take shortcuts now pay heavy consequences later when a marriage comes apart, a hidden untreated addiction becomes known, relationships suffer from neglect, professional growth stops, or spiritual temperature wanes, affecting us and those who take their lead from us.

All of us have a 'dark side.' The dark side includes those areas where we are vulnerable to temptation, places of unresolved emotional issues that spill out and hurt others, uncontrolled anger, selfishness that leads to narcissism, poor treatment of those we lead, or other issues that impact our lives and cause ruptures spiritually, emotionally or relationally. Dark sides must be dealt with. Otherwise they will cause us and others pain, and threaten our ability to lead.

Just as Christian leaders seek to understand God and His Word, they also need to understand themselves—areas of strength and areas of weakness. The better we understand how we are wired, how we are perceived, where we have blind spots and where and when we are vulnerable to sin, the healthier we will be because our awareness allows us to take those areas into account in our lives and leadership.

I have a good friend who pastors a church of 400 on the Gulf Coast. He is a good pastor. But he is also a driven guy, never content with where the church is, and not inwardly happy. He is constantly worried that the church is not growing the way it ought to be. Because he is insecure about his success as measured by church growth, he tends to be insecure when staff or board members differ with him on strategy or ministry priorities. The insecurity can show up as a defensive attitude.

My friend's dark side shows up in his discontent, lack of happiness, unquenchable drive and lack of self confidence. And it has an impact on his staff. If he is never content, he will never be content with what his staff does. If he is not internally a happy person, the lack of happiness will spill over on them. If he feels that success will be measured primarily by fast church growth, so will his staff.

These internal issues are unhealthy, cause my friend inner anxiety, cause conflict at times with the board due to defensiveness and lack of self confidence, and affects those he leads. In addition, his family pays the price as he is often mulling on his anxiety and not fully present for them.

Fortunately he is on a quest to figure out these issues which most likely can be traced back to his family of origin but which are spiritual issues as well. Unresolved, they will haunt him internally and affect his family and those he works with. The fact that he is now aware of the issues means that he can work on mitigating their effects on himself and others.

Understanding ourselves, our wiring, areas of temptation, strengths, weaknesses, motivations, dark sides and personal dysfunctions sets us on a path of personal growth and development which is crucial to leading well. The path is not always pleasant but it is necessary.

HI Moment:

Take 15 minutes and make some notes to yourself about your dark side. What lives in your dark side? What are you doing about it? How does it affect those around you? Are there areas that you need to pay attention to? What are you going to do about it? Do not neglect your dark side!

_____

_____

_____

_____

Those leaders who make the six areas of personal development central to their lives will develop the emotional, spiritual, relational and professional health they need to lead well.

Two: Strategic Leadership—
Providing strategic leadership to the organization
or the part of the organization you lead

In chapter one, we made the case that HI Teams are deeply missional. Leaders of HI Teams are the individuals who have the responsibility to keep missional issues in front of their team and to keep the team focused on strategies that will allow them to drive the mission forward.

This is not about administrating the team. There is a crucial difference between 'activity' and 'results.' Good leaders are always seeking results that are consistent with the mission. Leaders do some administration but they are not administrators. Rather, they are always pushing the mission forward—which often gets lost in the press of activity.

How do leaders provide strategic leadership? First, as team leaders they are the keepers of the vision for the team. They are the ones who always pull the team back to the mission. Without a leader who constantly reminds the team of its primary purpose, mission drift takes place and activity starts to replace results.

Second, leaders ask lots of questions: How can we do this better? What are others doing that we should know about? Are we all pulling in the same direction? Why do we do what we do the way we do it? Good leaders know that conventional wisdom and methods are often not productive and continually question their effectiveness.

Leaders are always asking questions, probing and looking for new ways of thinking about problems they face. One of my indicators of how good a leader someone is directly relates to how many questions they ask. Both one-on-one and in a team setting, leaders use questions to clarify issues, learn from others, and help come to workable solutions and new strategies. If this is not a natural trait, work on asking questions and you will be amazed at the results.

Leaders are also the ones who must regularly take a break from activity and do nothing but think! Busyness kills thinking time and strategic leadership means that someone is taking the time to simply think, ponder, muse and pray about the ministry they lead, the mission they have and how they can more effectively deliver on the mission. The tyranny of the urgent keeps many leaders and teams from being as effective as they could be if they just took the time to think.

Through meeting agendas, leaders keep the 'big rocks' or important issues in front of the team for discussion, problem solving, and collaborative strategy work. Because leaders set the agenda for their team, they determine how often the team focuses on strategic issues related to the mission and preferred future of the organization. This is why carefully planned and well-executed meetings are critical. What we do in meetings determines how missional the team is.

Leaders help their team determine what they do next to drive the mission forward. This involves key strategic initiatives that will provide significant leverage.[5] At any one time, every organization should be engaged in three-to-five strategic initiatives that are moving the mission forward.

Strategic leadership is about keeping the mission of the organization central and the team aligned toward accomplishing the mission. This is one of the core responsibilities of anyone who leads a team and must be scheduled into our priorities. Those of us who have served on ineffective teams know that it was often the result of leaders who did not take strategic leadership seriously and the team floundered.

Three: Strong Team—
Building a healthy, unified, aligned, strategic and results-oriented team

Newsflash: The higher the altitude at which you fly, the less you can do yourself and the more you are dependent on other people. Your ability to influence the organization you lead and advance the mission is directly dependent on the people who make up your team. Your success is tied directly to your team. So, the better the team, the more you will see accomplished.

Never underestimate the importance of strong team or underestimate your responsibility to build a healthy, unified, aligned, strategic and results-oriented team. We ignore strong team to our peril.

---

[5] For more information on strategic initiatives, see chapter 9 of *High Impact Church Boards*.

Why do I stress this so strongly? Because many leaders do not take team seriously! I have consulted with numerous churches, many of them large churches (attendance of 1,000 or more). The senior pastors are good communicators and often have great vision. Too often, however, they have ignored the building of strong team. Even if they have good people, the staff and leaders are often not unified around a common vision, in alignment with one another or with the senior pastor. Building strong team takes time and unless this becomes a priority of the team leader it will not happen. When it comes together, however, it is a dream and a joy to work with the team.

Strong team requires attention to four key areas. The first is getting the right people in the right seat. We will discuss this in the next chapter.

The second key to strong team is maximum missional clarity. When we are foggy on our mission, our vision or our preferred future, it is not possible to have alignment or missional unity because members are not sure what it is. Good leaders constantly work to clarify why we are here and where we are going. The more defining they are, the more aligned the team will be. Vince Lombardi, the famous football coach, would start each season with a simple lesson. He would hold up a football and say "this is a football." He started with the basics.

In chapter two, we saw how leaders can lead from the sandbox and keep their team aligned if they can clarify what the organization is really all about. What is your 'football?' Why does your team exist? What is the mission of your organization and team? Are all team members clear on what the end game is? If you live and talk the mission—all the time—those you lead will get it.

The third key to strong team is a willingness by the leader to empower team members to 'do their thing.' Micromanagement and control kill strong teams. Good people will not join or will leave teams where the leader controls them or their work. If you feel you must control your team—you either have the wrong people on the team, or you have a hard time empowering others.

I have a great friend who leads a very effective ministry that he founded. He is a classic entrepreneur/founder who feels a need to have his hand in everything in the organization. He is in need of key staff members but often when he hires at a senior level, the new staffers do not last long. It is not that he doesn't find good people.

The problem is that he does, and then these good people find that they have no freedom or empowerment to do what they were hired to do. Everything must be vetted by their founder and leader. Even though they love their leader and the mission of the organization, they find no joy in working in a disempowered environment.

When pastors like Jon come up with great new ideas that staff members must respond to (at the last minute), they disempower their staff who have been working diligently on their areas of responsibility. This does not mean that leaders cannot speak into 'what' or 'how' a team member is doing. The issue is how the leader does it so that the input empowers those on the team rather than disempowers them. Controlling leaders (and there are many) may attract good people if their vision is significant (good people love great vision), but they will not stay long term. Leaders who empower develop extremely loyal team members.

One of the issues related to empowerment is that of removing barriers that team members face which prevent them from carrying out their responsibilities. A barrier may be political, it may be an individual who is not playing ball, or it may be needed resources. Leaders remove barriers for team members that they cannot remove themselves. Every month I ask my team members two questions designed to get to this issue: "What do you need from me?" and "What barriers are you facing that you need to have removed?"

HI Moment:

Do you gravitate toward empowerment or control/micromanagement with your staff members? What do you think your team members would say? Can you think of any areas where you disempower your team? Are you willing to ask your team to respond to your level of empowerment?

The fourth key to a healthy, unified, aligned, strategic and results-oriented team is for the leader to take the posture of a mentor/coach. As a team leader, you are most likely the supervisor of those on the team.

What good people need is not primarily a supervisor but someone to coach and mentor them—or in the terms we use in our organization—develop, empower and release them. Team members need to know that their leader believes in them, wants the best for them, will develop them and empower them. Leaders who do this develop long term, loyal and healthy team members.

What is the cost? Our time! Mentoring and coaching means at least a monthly meeting and our availability when necessary. In a later chapter, we will discuss how to do this in an empowering way around Key Result Areas and an Annual Ministry Plan developed by your team members.

Remember the newsflash? While it takes time to be a mentor/ coach, the ministry results will be huge. Remember that your success is directly dependent on the success of those on your team. The more you pour into them, the more successful they will be. The more you empower them, the happier they will be. The more you clarify mission, vision and preferred future, the more motivated and aligned they will be. That is what mentor/ coaches do.

Four: Leadership Development— Develop current and future leaders

Pastors, church leaders and organizational leaders: are you developing current and future leaders for your ministry? It amazes me how many churches and organizations have no strategy or plan to develop future leaders and then wonder why they have trouble when new leaders come and create problems. Leaders pay close attention to identifying and developing new leaders for the future.

Good leaders, especially at higher organizational levels, are tough to find. As the leader of an organization of 500+ people spread across the globe, I am convinced that ReachGlobal will only be as good as the leaders it has. Why? Because good leaders attract the best people and they flourish under empowering leadership.

While I am blessed with a dream team in the two top leadership levels of the organization (and a great staff of missionaries), I am constantly asking three questions: "Who replaces these leaders if they were to leave?" "Where is my bench and who is on it?" and "What are we doing to intentionally find and develop potential leaders?" I will have failed if I do not raise up the next generation of leaders for the organization so that it flourishes in the future.

Whether you serve in a church setting or in another kind of ministry, there are significant advantages in raising new leaders from within your organization rather than going outside—when you can. Insiders know who you are, they understand your vision and mission, and they know the culture. Because they are insiders, you have the opportunity to develop and mentor them from the inside before they get into a leadership position. Of course, this is not always possible but developing your bench from within should be a key priority.

HI Best Practice:

Ask all team members to intentionally identify and develop someone who could take their place. In the best-case scenario you develop other qualified people for all key positions. In the event that a team member moves on, you have options available from inside the organization. Hold team members accountable for this on an annual basis.

In ReachGlobal, we have developed curriculum to intentionally develop new leaders for all key positions. I give personal attention to developing leaders for the two senior teams of the organization. In addition, we never meet as a senior team without a significant learning component included.

Remember, we will only be as good as the team who works for us. Do everything you can to build your current and future leaders and team members. I suggest that you have an articulated strategy for identifying and developing new team members, and make a place in your calendar on a periodic basis to review your progress against the strategy.

Five: Mobilizing Resources—
Mobilize key resources necessary
for the ministry of the team to flourish

Team leaders are mobilizers of:

- People
- Strategies
- Finances
- Other needed resources

Leaders use their authority, vision-casting ability and position in the organization to ensure that their team has the resources it needs to fulfill their responsibilities. This may mean negotiating with others at their level or higher for necessary budgets or cooperation. Sometimes it means finding donors to help fund specific ministry projects.

Mobilizing resources is not simply about funding, however. Leaders are 'people raisers,' always looking for individuals who can contribute to the mission. They are always on the lookout for strategies that might work or people who have been successful in what they are trying to do. All too often we try to 'reinvent wheels.' Leaders point their team to those who have already figured it out and encourage them to explore successful models.

What others have done in a particular area is a huge resource. Why pay 'dumb tax' that others have already paid? Why not learn from those who have figured out what you are trying to figure out? Leaders are always asking their team, "What do you need to get your job done?" Then they will help find the resources or point people in the right direction.

Resources can involve strategic partnerships with those who have expertise or ministry resources that can significantly help the team. They can include events where you bring together people who are trying to do what you are trying to do to exchange ideas and best practices. They may be groups of practitioners who can help your team think through opportunities they had not thought of.

One great untapped resource for ministry teams are professionals in the workplace who deal with issues as complex or more complex than we do. Engaging them to help us think strategically and find solutions to problems is huge leverage. Often they will think of solutions that we would never dream of because of their different perspective.

The central point is that we want to be networked with others, to know what is working, to understand 'pretty good practices,' rather than trying to reinvent the wheel or live in our own silo. Leaders help their team grapple with needed resources and point them in productive directions.

Everything we do as leaders of teams revolves around these five key areas of responsibility. Paying attention to them will help us lead well and will serve our team well.

A word to pastors regarding their boards

If you are a pastor and you are not yet practicing these five leadership responsibilities with your team, it is important that you have a conversation with your board to ensure that they will support the time and effort you will need to invest to do this well. Your ability to lead well depends on your investment in your team so it is crucial for your board to support that investment. You may want to have them read select chapters in this book.

HI Moment:

Leader's personal evaluation

- Are you comfortable with the fact that your team will only be as good as the leadership you provide?
- Where are you in the process of moving from individual producer to leading through team?
- In which of the five key responsibilities of a leader do you excel?
- Which of the five key responsibilities of a leader need more of your attention?
- Are you willing to dialogue with your team on these issues so that you can be a better leader for them?
- Are you flying at the correct altitude for you leadership role?

LEADER'S SCORECARD

Take a few moments and give yourself a grade (A, B, or C) in the following areas:

Transition from independent producer to leading through team _____

Intentionality in my spiritual life _____

Intentionality in my family life _____

Intentional growth in my professional life _____

Management of my 'dark side' _____

I regularly keep the mission in front of my team _____

I constantly ask questions _____

I regularly take time away to think _____

My team members are in the right seat _____

I provide maximum missional clarity to the team _____

I empower staff rather than control or micromanage _____

I intentionally mentor/coach my team members (at least monthly) _____

I have an intentional plan to develop new leaders _____

Mobilization of resources is high on my list _____

My schedule is designed to allow me to lead with excellence _____

CHAPTER SIX
Building a Healthy Team

HI Teams are deliberately built—over time.

Not all people are the right people for *your* team.

Potential or current team members can be categorized as A, B or C Team players. This is not about being a good or bad person, but about the ability to play well on your team. C Team players do not belong on your team no matter how 'nice' they are or how long they have been with you. They have a 'fatal flaw' that will compromise the work of the team.

In choosing team members, leaders never negotiate the crucial issues of character and good EQ. They take their time and pay the price to determine a good fit *before they hire* because they understand the principle: pay now or pay more later. They do not make hiring decisions alone.

In the hiring or recruiting process, leaders make the 'need to know' list of those things they must know about a potential team member, and those things that the potential team member needs to know about them, the team, and team expectations.

Healthy ministries are never static; therefore, good leaders continue to grow the capacity of the team through ongoing training. They are exegetes of the people they lead so that members are deployed in their 'sweet spot.'

Leaders build their team, one at a time, and build the capacity of the team through ongoing training. They never neglect the team!

HI Teams are deliberately built—over time. It is not an easy process and takes time and attention. But, the payoff is HUGE! The task of finding good people who fit your team and getting them into the right place is one of the most important things you will do as a leader. Nobody will get it right all the time, but if you can get it right most of the time your happiness factor will be high.

NOT ALL PEOPLE ARE THE RIGHT PEOPLE

While this seems obvious, many leaders do not spend enough time reflecting on who the right people are for their ministry. There are many good and competent people who will not fit *your* team. There are others who look great but who have fatal flaws that will cause you headaches. Getting the right people in the right seat affects two outcomes: growing the capacity of your ministry and avoiding unnecessary pain for you and the organization. If you lead a team, you have probably felt the pain!

A, B and C Team players

Potential or current team members can be categorized as A, B or C Team players. This is not about being a good or bad person, but about being able to play well on your team.

A Team players have qualities such as being self-directed, highly competent, committed to team and hard working. They are committed to your values and mission, require little management, and are results oriented. A Team players have high EQs, they work well with others and have good self awareness.

B Team players are committed to team, work hard, buy in to your values and mission, are results oriented, and have high EQ, but may require more direction. Generally, B Team players are not as creative or entrepreneurial as A Team players, but given concrete direction, they will do their jobs diligently and faithfully.

C Team players may or may not be competent (some are very competent and may even be 'stars'). But they have a *fatal flaw* that disqualifies them from serving on your team. Disqualifiers include lack of tangible results, laziness, lack of buy in or adherence to your mission or values, low EQ that disrupts relationships on the team or elsewhere, inability to work productively as a team player, or immaturity requiring constant management.

Let me boldly say what many in the Christian world are unwilling to say: C Team players do not belong on our teams no matter how 'nice' they are or how long they have been with you. To allow them to stay is to condemn the rest of the team to frustration and to compromise the mission of the organization. Remember, we are using God's resources to further God's Kingdom. We have a responsibility to our donors, to the Kingdom and to the mission of the organization to ensure that we deliver on that mission.

The question one needs to ask about C Team players is whether the fatal flaw can be dealt with so the individual can move from a C Team player to a B Team player. In one organization I consulted with, they had a brilliant individual who continually created relational problems for herself so that no one in the organization wanted to work with her. Yet her job was in a service division that required her to serve across departments.

There was no doubt as to her capacity, competency or agreement with the mission, but her low EQ was creating major issues of trust even for her boss (why didn't he do something?) and for the division he ran (they were delivering bad service). Even after executive coaching was undertaken at significant expense to the organization, behavior patterns did not change and they finally had to let her go. They probably should not have waited as long as they did as the relational chaos and subsequent lack of trust took several years to overcome.

It is possible that people operating at a C Team level in terms of results are in the wrong job (wrong seat) in which case you may want to do some testing and try an alternate job if one is available. What is not wise is to leave an incompetent person in place. Your credibility as a leader will be legitimately tarnished with the rest of your team if you do not deal with performance issues—or other fatal flaws.

Before you decide that someone is a C Team player, ask the question whether they have ever been coached or mentored. And, whether anyone has ever been honest with them regarding issues that are problematic. If not, you owe it to them to put them through a process to see if they can be retooled and brought up to a B Team level.

HI Best Practice:

Follow HR protocol in addressing performance issues with C Team players but once you know it is not going to change, act as quickly as you can to move them off of your team and out of your organization so that you minimize pain to the team and organization. Do so in a way that is gracious, defensible and as redemptive as possible but do not ignore the issue.

A and B Team folks are the heart of any good team and organization. In some higher-level jobs, you will need A Team players. In many jobs, a solid, faithful B Team player is exactly what you need. Know what you need and work to fill positions based on that need.

One of the realities of organizations is that someone who is an A or B Team player at one phase of an organization's life can slip to a B or a C at another. Most people have a built in "capacity ceiling" where they cease to be effective. Thus a youth worker who was a star when she had 20 youth in her group (she could personally relate to 20) starts to slip when she has 60 (she cannot relate to 60 and is not able to build team to help her).

It may be a case of not being able to multiply themselves so that they can lead a larger number of people or it may be they have just quit growing (an all too common scenario). If coaching and mentoring do not solve the issue, you may have to move them to another seat on your bus or help them, redemptively, find a seat on another bus. What you cannot do is allow someone to function at a sub-standard level without directly impacting the rest of your team and the results of the ministry. At any stage of your ministry's life, having the right people in the right seat is critical if the ministry is going to develop to the next level of effectiveness.

There are those who will think that what I have written here is harsh and lacking in grace. But think about this. Your first responsibility as a leader is to ensure the health of your organization while always acting redemptively when a change is needed. People who are not doing well are usually not in their sweet spot, and they often know it. To leave them there is not fair to the organization, to others on your team, and in the end, is not in the best interests of the one who cannot play at the level they need to play at.

Never negotiate the critical issues

Especially when hiring, it is a temptation to overlook character issues that may be present but are overshadowed by our view of a person's competency and what they might bring to our team. That is a fatal mistake for a leader in any organization, but especially in a Christian ministry where the character of our staff goes to the heart of our credibility. If there is any question on the character issue, walk away!

There are others who have great Christian character but don't have the right competencies or EQ. I am always amazed when someone who does not have the competencies or EQ is recommended for a position with the statement, "Well, they are really nice Christians and they want to work for a Christian organization." (For some, working for a nice Christian organization means that they could not make it in the secular world or are looking for personal needs to be met.)

Be clear on the Key Result Areas for the job as well as the competencies needed to fulfill the job

Job descriptions are not enough when you are looking to hire. Job descriptions describe the activities that the position entails. What you really need to focus on are the results you need to see for the activities. For all positions there ought to be three to five clearly defined results that, if fulfilled, will spell success (see chapter seven for more information on KRAs).

Once you know the results that spell success for the position you can determine the core competencies that you need for the individual to be successful. The core competencies are the non-negotiable skills that an individual *must possess* to successfully fulfill the Key Result Areas. Many things are negotiable in the hiring process and will be determined by the wiring and gifting of the individual. What are not negotiable are the core competencies since without these, there is no chance for the prospective hire to be successful.

Understand the principle: Pay now or pay more later

The longer I lead and the more people I hire, the more convinced I am of the wisdom of thorough testing before hiring (I've paid plenty of dumb tax for not doing it enough). The reason we don't do more testing and due diligence is that it costs money or we are in such a hurry to hire, or we choose to be optimistic and hope for the best.

Here is the reality. You either pay now and spend the time and money to ensure the competence of your potential hire, or you pay dearly later when you have to endure the pain of letting someone go—often after enduring months or years of performance issues. At the end of this chapter you will find a set of tests that can be helpful in learning about the wiring of your candidate.

If they will be playing at a senior level in the organization (including churches), it pays to put individuals through the same executive testing that any good secular organization would use. This will help measure capacity, leadership skills, conflict resolution skills and EQ. Untold pain and frustration would be avoided if we would take the long-term view and spend what we need to spend before we hire to ensure the best fit.

HI Best Practice:

Never make a hiring decision by yourself. Ask those who know you best and who have good discernment to interview those you are thinking of hiring. Do multiple interviews and listen to the gut reaction of those you bring into the process. Include interviewers that are both male and female to see how both react. Be wary of hiring if others you trust express cautions. They are probably seeing something you don't see (or don't want to see).

If you are hiring a senior individual in your ministry, consider going to their home and spending a day with the potential candidate. You will be amazed at what you learn about them, their marriage (if married) and their family relationships by doing so. Remember, pay now or pay more later!

A key reason for the best testing you can do is that you want to understand an individual's sweet spot before you hire them. Their sweet spot includes how they like to be managed, how they manage others, whether they like to work individually or in a team, what their driving values and passions are and where they have been successful in the past (past behavior is the best indicator of future behavior). The more you know about an individual's wiring, the better you will know how to coach and position them on your team.

Make the 'need to know' list

When you are adding someone to your team make two lists: what you need to know about the candidate and what they need to know about you. You need to know their wiring, background, competency, character, culture fit, work style, level they can play at, passions, values and whatever else is important to you.

You also need to make a list of what they need to know about you, your team, and your ministry. You don't want any surprises after you hire them and you don't want to surprise them either. They need to understand your leadership style, how you do team, expectations that you and the organization have, values, mission, preferred future of the organization, the culture of your ministry, what they can or cannot expect from you as the leader and other significant issues that define who you are as an organization. Be brutally transparent so that they know the upside and downside of your organization. If your honesty scares them away, they are the wrong hire.

HI Best Practice:

When you hire, have the candidate meet with and interview several people you currently lead who know you well so that they understand how you are wired, how you lead and what they can expect from you. Often those around us can give a better explanation of who we are and how we lead than we can ourselves.

It is wise to get references at least two layers deep so you can explore with those who know the candidate whether what you know about them is true and if they would fit your organization. You can expect the first list of references to be positive (the candidate gave them to you). Ask each of them for one or two additional names of people who would know the candidate well and contact the next layer. Never completely trust the feedback of references given to you by the candidate unless you personally know those references.

When discussing the fit of the candidate with references, be sure to describe to them the culture of the organization, the management and leadership style and the expectations. Someone may be competent but not fit your culture. Those who know the candidate best will be able to give feedback on the cultural and expectations fit.

Additional issues you want to explore before you hire, or reposition someone from within the organization onto your team are:

- Does this person have high EQ?
- Can this person play at the level that the other members of this team play at?
- Does this individual have a skill that will complement the team?
- Is this person a team player?
- Will they contribute to the whole rather than simply guard their turf?
- Do they fully embrace the mission and values of the organization?
- Do the other members of the team think they will fit well?
- Do they have the expertise needed for the ministry in which they will participate?
- Do they understand the implications of joining your team and what the expectations are for them as a team member?
- What level of leadership and management support will they need from you?
- If they will lead others, does their leadership style fit the leadership culture of the organization?

When hiring from the marketplace for a ministry role

I am a great fan of bringing good people from the marketplace into ministry organizations and have done it a number of times. However, there are sharp differences in culture between Christian organizations (and non-profits in general) and the marketplace that can complicate the marriage.

At the sake of oversimplification, the marketplace is often a bottom-line place (financial results), with less than collegial relationships (it's about the bottom line), has far more discipline for results (it's about the bottom line), and can be a rather unforgiving environment (which is why so many senior executives choose to retire early when they can). Fortunately there are exceptions where healthy work environments and healthy relationships are a priority.

Ministry organizations tend to be less driven by a bottom line (and less disciplined for results), are more collegial and gracious, and have a very different culture (for good or bad) than the marketplace does. Thus the transition from marketplace to ministry can be a shock to the system (for everyone). One of the search firms that I work with has watched this system shock many times and has come to the conclusion that coaching in the transition is critical.

One of my problematic hires was an individual who had worked for a major Fortune 500 corporation. When he interviewed he did very well but once on board, he managed to alienate almost everyone at his level or below with a crass, condescending attitude.

He never could cope with the collegial and gracious culture that our organization had (and he had a habit of being less than collegial). Several times he described to me the knock-down, verbal fights he observed among senior vice presidents with his previous employer (his idea of robust dialogue I guess). When I suggested that he be more collegial, his response was that we just were not "honest" in our organization. I said we were "honest, but gracious." After executive coaching did not change anything, he moved on to other pastures at our invitation.

One does not have to have an EQ issue like this individual to struggle with the transition from marketplace to ministry. It pays to be aware of the issues in such a transition and monitor the transition closely so that it goes well.

After the hire

You have your addition and you breathe a sigh of relief. But not too fast! Now, the real work begins. From day one, you want to ensure that your new team member understands the mission, values, preferred future and all the things you told them on your 'what they need to know' list. They have heard you, now you need to make sure that they 'get it' in terms of how they work on your team. The more personal time you can spend on the front end, the faster they will get up to speed and develop what you want them to develop rather than trying to figure out the 'rules' by watching others.

Set aside regular times to just sit with them over the first six months to ask them what they are observing, what they are surprised about, what information they need to do their job, and how you can remove barriers for them. Ask them how they read the culture of your team and ministry. They are new—you might be surprised by what they observe as a new set of eyes coming in. Probe with questions so that you both learn and can know how well they are assimilating into the organization. Make personal introductions to those they need to know in the organization.

For your own purposes and so you can do a better job with the next hire, after six months ask them to tell you what they wish they had been told on the front end, what the most difficult part of their transition was and what was most helpful in the entire process. Jot down their feedback and incorporate it into your next hiring process.

GROWING YOUR TEAM'S EFFECTIVENESS

Building strong team is never finished which is why it is one of the five ongoing responsibilities of a leader. Healthy ministries are never static—they grow and expand and therefore the effectiveness of the team you lead must continue to grow with the ministry. Only one person—the team leader—can ensure that this happens.

The ongoing training of your team ought to be tied to the initiatives you are driving in any given year. While there are many areas you can help your team develop, the most critical areas will be the ministry initiatives that the organization (or your part of the organization) is driving so that there is alignment between the organization's needs and your team's capacity.

Our organization recently trained all personnel in the use of Annual Ministry Plans tied to Key Result Areas. This meant that it was critical to train our senior team first and then to train all supervisors in the skills needed to become mentor/coaches. These two areas became the focus of our ongoing training with our two top teams since the skill of our leaders was tied to the organization's initiative to help all personnel become more intentional in their work. It is our practice to determine several important areas of needed training for our senior teams each year and develop a strategy to carry it out. If you have several key teams in your organization, you will want to ensure that ongoing development is coordinated for all your teams.

HI Best Practice:

Regularly build into your team's agenda major blocks of time for learning together, including dialogue around those topics you are covering. Keep a list of the training you have done, along with the resources you have used. As new members join your team, ensure that there is a plan for them to 'get up to speed' on issues you have covered so that they will be in sync with the rest of the team.

KEY TOPICS FOR TEAM LEARNING TOGETHER

While much team learning will be specific to the kind of organization you are and the ministry initiatives you are driving, there are some areas of training that all healthy teams will pay attention to. These have to do with leadership, sweet spots, emotional intelligence, team dynamics, and learning how to live and minister intentionally rather than accidentally.

Leadership

HI Teams do a great deal of training in the area of healthy leadership. The more leaders you can develop in your organization the stronger you will be. The ability of team members to lead well at their level is crucial.

Necessary skills include how to be a collaborative leader, how to clarify the mission, values, preferred future and ministry initiatives of the organization, and the ability to mentor and coach those they lead. Some of these issues will be covered later in this book. At the end of this chapter you will also find resources that can help grow your team's leadership skills.

Sweet spots

Leaders are exegetes of the people they lead. Too often we simply see people as filling a slot in our organization rather than finding the best people we can and building their job around the gifting and skills that God has given them. When someone is in the right seat and they are in a place where they will be successful because the seat was designed for them, they are in their sweet spot.

HI Best Practice:

Find the best people you can and then build their responsibilities around the gifting and wiring that they have so they will be most effective and happy in their work. The bottom line is their ability to fulfill the KRAs of their area of responsibility. How they accomplish the work will depend on their wiring.

In the absence of paying attention to a person's sweet spot and playing to their strengths, people are frustrated and not as productive as if they were positioned for maximum effectiveness (and joy) in their work. As a team leader, one of my core missions is to help position the great people who work on my team in the place where they will be most effective. That means that I must watch them, dialogue with them, be willing to modify their job descriptions and do all I can to keep them engaged.

How do we determine our own (or others') sweet spots? Consider asking these questions:

- What things fill my tank and what things deplete me?
- What things do I love to do and which do I put off?
- What am I most effective at and what am I either marginally effective at or really poor at?
- If I could design my perfect job description it would be....
- How do others evaluate my areas of strength and weakness?
- If I could change one thing about my current job that would make my job a lot more fulfilling, what would it be?

For many years, conventional wisdom was that one ought to work on strengthening one's weaknesses. We now know that it is far wiser to focus on our strengths than to try to fix our weaknesses. In fact, people will be the most productive if they can spend no more than 20-40% percent of their time in areas of weakness and 60-80% in areas of strength. We need to help people design their responsibilities in ways that maximize their strengths and find other ways to support their weaknesses.

If someone is really in the wrong spot (they are not playing to their strengths) it may be necessary to help them find another seat on the bus or if there is not another seat on your bus, a seat on another bus.

Helping those on your team understand the sweet spot concept will then allow them to apply the same thinking to those whom they lead. People who are in the right seat and playing to their strengths are happy and productive.

Emotional intelligence

In the previous chapter we discussed the importance of understanding who we are, our areas of strength and our dark side. We defined Emotional Intelligence (often labled EQ), as the ability to understand ourselves, what drives us, how we are perceived by others, how well we relate to others and whether we have the relational skill to work synergistically with others while being both self defining and allowing others to speak into our lives or work without defensiveness.

Because good EQ plays such an important role in the corporate effectiveness of the team and for each of your team members individually, ongoing discussion and training in these areas becomes significantly important. In the church, for instance, more conflict and misunderstandings are caused by poor EQ than by anything else. We cannot expect members of the congregation at large to always display high EQ, but those who are on staff must.

If a team member consistently demonstrates poor EQ—resulting in relational issues with other members of the team or those they serve—you may need to provide coaching and if that does not work, help them find another place to work.

Team dynamics

Remember the definition of team: "A group of missionally aligned and healthy individuals working strategically together under good leadership toward common objectives with accountability for results." This is not possible unless there is health on the team in how they work and relate to one another and how they see their role on the team. In chapter one, I defined the characteristics of a healthy team and these are areas that dialogue and training must be geared to on an ongoing basis.

Intentional living and intentional ministry

In the next chapter we will look at a paradigm for ensuring that the lives and ministries of those we lead are deeply intentional. On the ministry side, this is a non-negotiable if one is going to develop HI Teams and leaders. This intentionality must be an ongoing topic of discussion because it is easy for teams to revert to activity rather than stay focused on results.

Keep team members from 'leadership default'

There is a principle about teams that is often overlooked and frequently violated. Simply stated, the senior team that we serve on is our most important team and is the team of our first allegiance.

For those of us who *serve on a team* and *lead a team* this is an important distinction. The senior team I currently serve on is the senior team of a denomination. The team I lead is the senior team of the global ministries of that denomination. Which of these teams demands my highest loyalty? The senior team I serve on or the team I lead? It is always the senior team that I serve on, which in this case, is the senior denominational team.

Why? Because the global ministry team I lead is *under the organizational authority* of the senior team I serve on. Thus the senior team requires my highest loyalty. That means that while I lead a team, everything I do with 'my' team is always in alignmnent with the senior team. I am *first* a spokesman for the senior team rather than first being an *advocate* for the team I lead.

Understanding and living out this principle prevents conflicts between the two teams and ensures organizational alignment because my loyalty to the senior team ensures that I lead 'my' team from the perspective of the senior team. In my leadership of the global team, I am first and foremost a spokesperson for the senior denominational team. As such I will never allow the team I lead to develop an 'us/them' mentality with the senior team, nor will I ever criticize the decisions or direction of the senior denominational team (I helped make them). Remember, I am first and foremost a spokesperson for the senior team on which I serve.

Some leaders push back on this position thinking that it limits their ability to have robust discussion on their team or to deal with issues that affect their team. Not so. The issue is *where* I deal with the issues. On the senior team, I have all the opportunity in the world to deal with issues that potentially impact my team. But that is the correct place for me to air them. Once I leave that room, I am a spokesperson for any decisions made there. With the team I lead, I have an obligation to explain, support, defend and finesse those decisions so that those I lead can understand and work within the parameters of decisions made above our team. Not to do so is to create deadly divisions within the organization that *hurt* the organization and its ministry, and negatively impacts its missional effectiveness. If we cannot *follow well* we cannot *lead well*.

Let's apply this to the church. In most churches, the senior pastor is on the leadership board of the church. This would be his or her senior team which would demand their highest loyalty. They would typically then lead a staff team. If they understand this principle, they would never take a position with their staff against direction or policies of the board. To do so is to engage in 'leadership default' with a resulting us/them mentality and to have violated their first loyalty and responsibility.

At the same time, those staff members who serve on the senior pastor's team must realize that this is their senior team and they cannot allow the teams they lead to be at odds with the senior staff team. As leaders they are always first and foremost spokespersons for that senior staff team rather than being 'advocates' for the team they lead. Not only is this good leadership but it prevents an us/them mentality which is all too common in ministry organizations.

The neglect of this principle causes no end of conflict between boards and senior staff or between senior staff teams and lower level ministry teams in a church or organization. It is an authority issue, an alignment issue and a leadership issue. This does not mean that there is not healthy, robust discussion on any team. What it does mean is that the team leader will not default in his or her leadership by allowing their team to be out of alignment with the senior team they are on (the team above).

A TRUE STORY

Some time ago I met with a team of leaders from an area of the world whose leader serves on *my* senior team. What I did not realize was that these leaders had a number of questions about the ministry direction we were taking and when they asked *their* senior leader about them he said "you will have to ask T.J. about that." The message sent to those he leads was, therefore, *I can't answer that* [he should have been able to answer that], *you need to talk to T.J.* [the Executive Director] giving the impression that he (a member of my team) was unwilling to take the same ownership for the direction as I did. Remember, he serves on my team and was part of all discussions on the directional decisions we made.

In the meeting, his leaders peppered me with questions from a 'we/you' perspective while their leader listened and did not take a position that 'I am with T.J. on this and this is where *we* are going.' My team member had engaged in leadership default, choosing to identify more with the team he led than with the senior team he was on, creating an unhealthy situation where he allowed an us/them mentality to develop.

Signs of leadership default include:

- Siding with your team over or against the senior team you are on—either directly or by implication. This often happens when a team leader needs to be popular with those he or she leads and therefore, does not want to take ownership of a decision he or she was actually a part of.
- Blaming others for decisions your senior team was a part of. For instance, if a pastor blames the board for a decision that is unpopular with staff, he/she has engaged in leadership default because as a member of the board he should always own the decision as 'ours,' not 'theirs.'
- Not fully supporting and actively defending a decision or direction with the team one leads made by the senior team one is on.

Leadership default hurts organizations and sets one level of leadership against another level. When we follow the principle, there is alignment within the organization and we are not setting one group against the other or guarding our turf (the only turf should be the missional turf of the whole organization). Living out this principle would prevent most of the us/them mentality of boards against staff or ministry teams against staff. Those who reject this principle have not learned how to follow well and those who cannot follow well are not fit to lead.

HI Best Practice:

Ensure that members of your team understand that the senior team they serve on is their most important team and it is the team of their first allegiance. If they engage in leadership default address it quickly. If it becomes a regular practice, be defining that the behavior hurts the organization and that it must stop.

THE SPIRITUAL COMPONENT OF HI MINISTRY TEAMS

This book is written for ministry teams who by definition are committed to building Christ's Kingdom. For those of us who have the privilege of serving in this arena, the wisdom, empowerment and favor of God becomes deeply important in all that we do together. In saying this I am not making a distinction between those who serve Christ in the secular arena and those who do so in the ministry arena. The difference is that 'as a team' in a ministry organization there is opportunity to tap into the power of God on a regular basis.

Just as I believe that the spiritual life of church leaders is indispensible to their leadership role, so I believe that the spiritual life of ministry teams is inseparable from their ability to minister well and lead well in their areas of responsibility. As Jesus said in John 15:5, *"without me you can do nothing,"* of lasting spiritual fruit. The corollary is that *"If you remain in me and I in you, you will bear much fruit, fruit that will last."* (John 15:16)

Asking the Father to speak into our strategies, give us wisdom and empower what He places in our hearts is vital to work as a team. Furthermore, what we model with our team in terms of spiritual dependence will be modeled by our team members in working with those they lead and will have a cascading effect throughout the organization.

COMMUNICATIONS AS A MATRIX IN THE FLAT WORLD

Communication builds trust and trust minimizes conflict because information is power. The issue of how an organization designs systems where the right information gets to the right people at the right time so that good decisions can be made and everyone knows what *they* need to know is complex. When it comes to information, everyone has an opinion and expectations are hard to meet. Some common complaints I hear are:

- We don't get enough information
- We get too much information
- I don't know everything that is happening
- You did not solicit my opinion or input before you made that organizational decision

- My leaders don't tell me what is going on at their level
- Leaders can cascade information *down* through the organization but how do I send information back *up* to them?

These are real issues in the development of healthy organizational cultures and healthy teams. There are some principles that if understood and practiced would help address these and similar concerns.

In today's flat world, communication is from the top down, the bottom up and horizontal all at once

While there must be intentional organizational communication, the day of leaders simply telling the organization what it needs to know is long gone. I receive up to 100 emails per day, from people throughout our organization, from national ministry partners, from donors and pastors on any number of issues. And, I reply to every one of them or I ensure that the one who can address the issue they have raised replies to them.

One of the great blessings of our day is the access to information from many sources and the ability for most to quickly communicate throughout the organization to share insights, express opinions, offer solutions or share challenges. This works both ways. In the traditional top-down organizational structure, employees knew primarily what their leaders wanted to tell them. And, leaders knew primarily what their reports chose to pass back to them. No longer: I can solicit or receive unsolicited information from anywhere in the organization and so can anyone else in the organization.

In today's flat world, it is the responsibility of every team member to share information that needs to be shared with whom it needs to be shared and to solicit needed information in order to make healthy decisions.

Here is a paradigm shift. In the old paradigm, it was primarily the job of leaders to communicate pertinent information throughout the organization. In the flat world, it is the job of *everyone* to share relevant information that they possess to those who need to know it *regardless* of where they fit in the organization.

And, it is the responsibility of each of us to solicit information we need (if we don't have it) from those who do have it to make the best-possible decisions. Rather than allowing a culture of blame to exist (you didn't tell me), we need to create cultures of proactive communication in which people at all levels of the organization are responsible to others at all levels of the organization. This is empowering for those who practice it because anyone, at any level of the organization has the ability to influence the direction of the organization if they are willing to share what they know or solicit the information they need to know to do their job well.

Flat organizations that are intentionally healthy create an egalitarian communications culture where everyone has the responsibility and freedom to communicate with those who need information they have and to solicit information they need. At the same time they retain organizational structure and accountability and the support for decisions by the right people at the right level of the organization. The central theme here is that every one of us has responsibility to communicate relevant information, not just some of us.

Not everyone needs to know everything

Small organizations are like families. In families, everyone kind of knows what everyone is kind of doing. It happens naturally through family relationships, shared meals and relational proximity. As organizations grow, this changes because of the complexity of ministries, relationships, the number of personnel and the need for everyone to focus on their particular areas of responsibility.

For those who were in the organization when it was small, this is a tough transition because where they always used to be in the know, they no longer are. This is a painful transition for staff members in growing churches.

Historically, the organization I lead has called itself a family. And, back in the '60s when the denomination was small and the mission family was small, it felt like a family. Today it is not a family but an organization because you cannot be 'family' with 550 personnel scattered across 40 countries of the world. Thus, like a church that has grown out of the family stage (at about 150 people), we have as well but the expectation is still there by some (who remember the old days) to think we are family.

As organizations grow, members of the organization become more focused on their area of responsibility rather than on the whole. A family knows what is going on with all its members, a clan does not. When people say to me, "I don't know everything that is happening anymore," I reply, "neither do I." The truth is I need to know *certain things*, but *not* a lot of things. I expect members of the organization to share significant breakthroughs or issues, and always their concerns. But much of what happens I don't know. I am trusting good people to do the right thing. *Anyone who expects to know everything, or even most things in a growing organization, will be disappointed by their unrealistic expectation.*

In a flat organization *everyone* has responsibility for communication:

- To communicate concerns to appropriate people
- To communicate with appropriate parties after decisions are made
- To solicit information that is needed for making wise decisions from any level of the organization
- To alert leadership of barriers, concerns and opportunities
- To be as transparent as possible on any issues that are raised
- To recognize that no one will know everything
- To take personal responsibility for getting information they need rather than complaining that they did not get it

SUMMARIZING DECISIONS AND ASSIGNMENTS

Without someone keeping notes of decisions and assignments, team meetings are sloppy and accountability is difficult. Choose someone on your team who has an administrative gift and give them the responsibility to record decisions and assignments that are immediately sent to all team members after a meeting.

Before you close the meeting, have them summarize what they recorded to ensure everyone hears the same thing. They should then work with the team leader to build the agenda for the next meeting to ensure appropriate follow up on assignments. Remember, execution on missional decisions is what counts.

HI Best Practice:

Never end a team meeting without summarizing cascading information, decisions and assignments. Immediately after the meeting, distribute these to the team.

RULES OF ENGAGEMENT

Every team has rules, written or otherwise, by which they operate. These rules can be healthy or unhealthy. Unhealthy rules include certain topics that everyone knows are off limits (the elephants), or might be that nothing can ever be said that the leader might take as critical. Some teams are great at process but do not deal with accountability or results. Unhealthy rules prevent teams from having candid, honest, robust dialogue.

Only the leader can truly set the tone or culture of a team. Others can try but the leader has the authority to either encourage a culture or discourage it. The more a leader defines the team 'rules of how we work with each other' and then models that culture, the greater the freedom the team has to operate comfortably with each other. The following rules of engagement would typify a healthy team. It takes healthy emotional intelligence on the part of the leader and those on the team to make this possible.

TEAM COVENANT

- We encourage robust dialogue where honest opinions, probing questions and potential solutions can be freely shared on any topic relating to the team's (or one another's) ministries. We commit to robust dialogue without attacking one another and to maintain an open, non-defensive attitude.

- In the spirit of Matthew 18, we will always speak in love and keep short accounts when offence has taken place.

- We will regularly evaluate progress of the organization or that part of the organization we are responsible for and do so with utmost honesty. We believe in timely execution and ministry results.

- We practice autopsy without blame. We know things will go wrong and when they do we will do an autopsy of the failure so that we can learn from it without casting blame for the failure.

- We keep our promises. When decisions have been made and assignments given, we are committed to fully executing those assignments on time.

- We take full responsibility for corporate decisions our team makes and will not engage in leadership default. Our first loyalty is to this team and we will always represent this team well and fully support its decisions. Outside of our team meetings we speak with one voice.

- We keep confidential those issues which are shared in our team meetings which should not be shared with others.

- We are committed to thinking the best of one another, speaking the best of one another, praying for one another and supporting one another's ministries.

- We agree to hold one another accountable for keeping this team covenant and we agree to allow others to call us on it if we violate this agreement.

HI Moment for Those Who Lead Others:

- As you think through those on your team, who are the A, B, and C Team players?
- Are there any team members who are either in the wrong spot or who should not be on your team?
- What do you need to do differently in choosing team members in the future?

HI Moment for Team Discussion:

- What areas could we improve if we were to 'do team' better?
- Which areas in the team covenant do we practice well? Which do we violate?
- What areas of team effectiveness mentioned in this chapter would we like to do further study on as a team?

RECOMMENDED READING
FOR UNDERSTANDING WHO YOU ARE

Guinness, Os, The Call: *Finding and Fulfilling the Central Purpose of Your Life,* Thomas Nelson, 2003, ISBN: 0849944376

Kise, Jane A., Stark, David, and Hirsch, Sandra Krebs, Lifekeys Discovery Workbook: *Discovering Who You Are, Why You're Here, and What You Do Best*, Baker Publishing Group, 2005, ISBN: 0764200763

Rath, Tom, StrengthsFinder 2.0: *A New and Updated Edition of the Online Test from Gallup's Now, Discover Your Strengths*, Gallup Press, 2007, ISBN: 159562015X

Winseman, Albert L., Clifton Donald O., and Liesveld, Curt, Living Your Strengths: *Discover Your God-Given Talents and Inspire Your Community*, Gallup Press, 2004, ISBN: 1595620028

RECOMMENDED SELF-KNOWLEDGE TOOLS

Clifton StrengthsFinder

The Clifton StrengthsFinder assessment tool measures a person's talent. This tool is a starting point for self discovery. http://www.strengthsfinder.com/

DiSC

The DiSC Classic Profile tool measures behavioral personality. This assessment provides an understanding of people through increased awareness of temperament and behavioral styles. http://www.internalchange.com/

Keirsey-Bates Temperament Sorter

The Keirsey Temperament Sorter II® (KTS®-II) is a 70-question personality instrument that helps individuals discover their personality type. http://www.advisorteam.org/

Uniquely You Spiritual Gifts Inventory

This tool combines spiritual gifts with the 4 DISC personality types. http://www.uniquelyyou.com/

CHAPTER SEVEN
The Power of Intentional Living

The key distinction of HI Teams is the intentionality with which leaders and individuals live their lives and pursue their ministries.

People who see significant results of their work think differently than others. Rather than focusing on *activity*, they focus on *results*. They have chosen intentional living over accidental living.

Key Result Areas help us determine the desired results of our work. They answer the question, 'what is success?' They allow us to focus on the critical rather than being driven by the urgent. They help us prioritize and say no to good but non–critical activities.

Annual Ministry Plans are the specific steps we are going to take in any given year to fulfill Key Result Areas. They give us a paradigm for thoughtfully and prayerfully thinking through what needs to be done and how we will do it. They help us stay on task and measure our progress.

Connecting our Key Result Areas and Annual Ministry Plans to our calendar is 'connecting the compass to the clock.' It is the linchpin between good planning and good execution on those plans.

Good leaders and HI Teams choose to live and work with great intentionality and accountability.

They choose intentional living over accidental living.

The key distinction between HI Teams and other teams is the intentionality with which leaders and individuals live their lives and pursue their ministries. We live in a day of huge needs, multiplied demands, out-of-control schedules and the tendency to be driven by the urgent, not the most important. Over time, our effectiveness is eroded, our hearts become tired and we know deep down that there must be a better way to live life and pursue ministry.

Three observations ought to give us pause. First, we are all busy. When people describe to me how busy they are and how fast they run in ministry, I am not impressed. Everyone is busy.

Second, we are all busy but not everyone sees the same results. Some people are exceedingly productive while others accomplish little.

Third, activity does not equal results. This is a critical distinction. Busyness does not equal results. That is why I am unimpressed with how packed one's schedule is. The question is not how much activity we are involved in, but what the results are of our life and work. Activity that is not strategic yields little for the energy expended and leaks away opportunity for Kingdom results.

People who see significant results of their work think differently than others. Rather than focusing on activity, they focus on results. They have identified the results they want to see for their lives and then strategically focused their activity toward those results. They are highly discriminating in what they do, the obligations they agree to, and how they schedule their days. Before they say "yes" to new opportunities they think and pray, determine whether the activity will contribute to what they understand to be the big rocks of their lives, and practice the power of saying "no."

HI Definition:

Intentional Living is the discipline of knowing how God made us, defining the big rocks in our life and work, and executing with an intentional annual plan that connects our schedules with the big rocks in a way that maximizes our God–given gifting and call.

ACCIDENTAL AND INTENTIONAL LIVING

All of us live somewhere on a continuum between accidental and intentional living. I have contrasted the difference between the two styles of living in the chart below. Look carefully at the column on the left (accidental) and then the column on the right (intentional).

Accidental vs. Intentional Living

Accidental	Intentional
• Lives moment by moment	• Lives within structure
• Often harried	• Seldom harried
• Little advanced planning	• Significant advanced planning
• Does not distinguish between 'big rocks' and 'small rocks'	• Distinguishes between critical and non-critical
• Busy without well defined priorities	• Schedule revolves around key priorities
• Allows life to determine schedule	• Mission drives schedule

HI Moment:

Take a moment and mark those characteristics that best describe how you live your life. Do you fall more on the accidental or the intentional side of the continuum? Are you pleased with where you are?

How intentionally we live our lives matters. From a personal perspective, the issue is whether we are using the gifts, time and opportunities Christ has given to us to the fullest advantage. We have one life to live and it goes fast. On the other side of 50, I am on the down slope of opportunity, time-wise, but have greater opportunity to influence others given my stage of life and the lessons I have learned.

I meet few individuals who want to squander their lives, yet the way they go about life does not match their desires. Lack of careful thinking about priorities and schedules, allowing others to determine them, and not living in light of the gifts and opportunities God has given us equal accidental living.

In John 15, Jesus makes it clear that fruit matters to God. Our lives are not only to bear fruit, but much fruit, fruit that will last. The fruit of our lives is directly related to the gifting God has given us and the "work that he prepared in advance for us to do." (Ephesians 2:10) Seeing the reality of this fruit is directly related to how intentionally we live our lives in light of our God-given gifting and priorities. All things being equal, the choices we make are the crucial difference between those who accomplish much and those who accomplish less.

HI leaders and teams are made up of people who refuse to settle for accidental living, out-of-control schedules, unfocused activity or the expectations of others. Rather, they are deeply thoughtful about what God has called them to accomplish, focusing strategic activity on the big rocks of their lives, all of which come out of a deep sense of God's call and our stewardship of that call.

OVERWHELMING DESIRES AND UNDERWHELMING PLANS

Everyone wants their lives to count. No one reading this book wants to squander the opportunity they have to influence our world for Christ. We have an overwhelming desire for significance. But, many of us have an underwhelming plan for how to accomplish our desire!

Unless we develop an intentional plan and an ongoing life rhythm we will not fulfill our desire for lives of significance. Let's face it, accidental living is an easy default position because it takes no intentionality or discipline. Intentional living takes discipline and there is a price to pay for it. The price includes doing the hard work of understanding what God has called us to accomplish, how we are wired and the discipline to strategically focus our activity toward those big rocks that spell success for our lives and work. Those who do the hard work and live their lives with discipline see far more fruit than those who don't.

HI Teams organize their work in ways that insist that all members are living (at least in the work place) with a huge degree of intentionality. There is a focus on results, on strategically focused activity and a rhythm that keeps everyone aligned with one another and the mission of the team. It is a deeply satisfying place to be.

LEGACY

Fast-forward your life to the day of your funeral. Your family is there, as well as your friends and colleagues. What are they saying about your life? What are your children remembering? Your spouse! Those who knew you best? If there were a handful of things you would want to be known by, what would they be?

HI Moment:

At the end of my life I would want people to remember me for:

_____

_____

_____

_____

_____

Assume that you have five years left in your current ministry. If you could accomplish three-to-five things that leave a lasting influence, what would they be? Take a moment and write them down.

_____

_____

_____

_____

_____

What you have just identified are the big rocks of your life. They are the key results that you want your life and your work to have. Getting these big rocks right is one of the most important things we can do if we are going to live intentionally and focus on results. If we don't know the big rocks, we don't know where to focus our activity.

HI Moment:

Take another moment and answer this question for each of the big rocks you listed above for your life and work. How strategically is my activity aligned with the few key results I want for my life and work? Be honest with yourself.

KEY RESULT AREAS

KRAs are Key Result Areas. Understanding of and commitment to KRAs is a major contributor in moving from activity to focused living. Much of what we have been taught or seen modeled that is related to how we structure our lives, focuses around activity. For instance, most job descriptions are a description of the activities that the job entails. The message is that if one carries out the activities found in the job description they will have been successful in their work. But it is not true!

There is a major fallacy here because activity does not equal results. There are many people whose work lives are filled with activity but there is not much to show for it. All of us are busy with activity but activity is not the relevant issue.

KRAs help us determine the desired results of our work

The key to intentional living is being able to clearly identify what the results of our work and life ought to be rather than the activity that the job entails. That was the point of the exercises above.

HI Definition:

Key Result Areas are the specific results that spell success for us in our job and life. KRAs do not spell out *how* we will achieve those results (activity) but describe the *definition of success* (results). KRAs define the critical areas of success that one must *achieve* if one is going to be *successful* in one's work.

KRAs answer the question, 'What is success?'

Because KRAs define what success looks like, they cut through the clutter of activity and get to the heart of the matter—what our activity must lead to. They answer the question of success and are applicable in both our personal and professional lives. KRAs do not define activity, goals or methods. They define the end result of our work, the ultimate outcome that we want to see in any given year. Goals and methodology come after we have defined our KRAs.

Why KRAs? Key Result Areas allow us to focus on the critical rather than be driven by the urgent. They clarify the non-negotiable priorities and allow us to make decisions about our time and energy on the basis of a set of clear outcomes that will allow us to fulfill God's call on our lives.

Think of all the demands on your time. Some of those demands come from others who love to tell you what is important for you and how you should spend your time. All of us have options and opportunities as to what we could do with our time and we face regular pressures to fulfill the expectations of others. We face the challenges:

- How do we prioritize?
- How do we schedule?
- What gives us the confidence to say yes or no?
- Where do we focus?
- How do we deal with competing voices?
- How do we free ourselves from the tyranny of the urgent?

The answer is to identify your Key Result Areas. They become your key focus and priorities and the grid from which you can answer these questions.

Think back to the priorities of a leader spelled out in chapter five. These are Key Result Areas that spell success as a team leader. If these five areas are *not* accomplished, the team leader *cannot* be successful. Note that they do not spell out methods or strategies, rather they define the end result of their team leadership:

- ***Personal Development:*** *Ensuring that I live an intentional life in my spiritual, family, emotional, relational and professional life.*
- ***Strategic Leadership:*** *Providing strategic leadership to the organization or the part of the organization that I lead.*
- ***Strong Team:*** *Building a healthy, unified, aligned, strategic and results-oriented team.*
- ***Leadership Development:*** *Develop current and future leaders.*
- ***Mobilizing Resources:*** *Mobilize key resources necessary for the ministry of the team to flourish.*

If a team leader can successfully keep his or her life on track, provide the right strategic leadership to the team, build a strong and healthy team, develop current and future leaders, and mobilize needed resources, they will be successful as leaders. They may have additional Key Result Areas, but these five are non-negotiable for those who lead teams.

HI Moment:

Take a few minutes and think through the Key Result Areas that would spell success for you in your job. Do not include methodology or action steps, but answer the question, 'What things do I need to accomplish to successfully do my job?' Share these conclusions with other members of your team and invite their input. Do they agree that this is what success would look like?

1._____

2._____

3._____

4._____

5._____

The reason this is important is that unless you can clearly define success (and have your supervisor's agreement that it spells success), you will not know how to channel your activity. KRAs spell out the goal of our work and energy—they define the focus of our activity and define success.

KRAs help us prioritize

Once I understand what my Key Result Areas are, it becomes the grid through which I can measure all of my demands and opportunities. In my role I have many opportunities to attend far-flung meetings, to speak, or to be involved on various boards. I also have many people who would like to determine my priorities for me—so that they align with theirs. It would be easy to say "yes" to good but non-essential activities, either because I enjoy doing them (well the meeting was in Greece after all!) or because I felt the pressure of others to accept.

How do I determine whether I should say "yes" or "no?" From my KRAs! As I say to my team, "there are lots of things I could do as your leader but if I do not accomplish these things (my KRAs), the organization will suffer and I will have failed as a leader." Through my KRAs, I have an extraordinary amount of clarity regarding my priorities. And these priorities take precedence over everything else.

Having maximum clarity around one's KRAs allows one to:

- Develop an annual plan around those priorities
- Choose opportunities on the basis of the KRAs
- Have the freedom to say "no" or "yes"
- Differentiate between competing voices and agendas
- Delegate to others areas that are not our prime responsibility
- Stay focused on the main thing for our lives

KRAs should be within our sweet spot and reflect what we believe God's call on our life to be. Having determined them and having the agreement of our supervisor, we have the freedom to focus on those few areas that both become our priorities and which spell success in our lives and jobs.

THE POWER OF NO

There is an interesting passage about Jesus in Mark 1:21-39. Jesus was in Capernaum where he healed Simon's mother-in-law, and "healed many who had various diseases. He also drove out many demons." Early the next morning Jesus went to a quiet place to pray. When Simon and his companions found Jesus, they told Him "Everyone is looking for you!"

Jesus' response is surprising. Rather than doing what the disciples expected, and going to those looking for Him, He replied, "Let us go somewhere else—to the nearby villages—so I can preach there also." In other words, He said *no* to the need and expectations the disciples brought to Him because he had more important missional things He needed to do. Jesus understood the power of "no" because He could distinguish between those things that were *good* and those things that were *critical* for His ministry. Jesus was *self defining* about what He needed to do rather than allowing others to define those things for Him.

It should not be lost on us that Jesus said "no" to the disciples' expectation after He had spent time with His Father. Jesus was in the habit of regularly taking time to refresh His intimacy with the Father and to pray through those things He should be doing so that His priorities were in alignment with the priorities of the Father.

Most of us love to please others. It makes us feel good because in saying "yes" to others' requests they feel good about us and we feel good about ourselves. We get our cookies by pleasing others!

I once did a consultation with a senior pastor of a large church. I was there because his staff felt he did not pay enough attention to them and to building a strong team. When I probed the pastor about how he spent his time (activity), one of the things I learned was that he made *all* the hospital calls—in a large church! When I asked why he said, "Because it makes me feel good." At least he was honest. While his activity was 'good,' it was not focused on what his true big rocks were, which included building a strong staff team (results). His team was suffering because of his focus on the wrong activity—for him.

Yes and *No* are powerful words with powerful results. Saying "yes" to the right things allows us to focus our attention on those key areas that spell success for us. Saying "no" to the wrong things (nice activity that is not strategic for what God has called us to do) is equally powerful. God has called each of us to a few Key Result Areas in our lives. Lots of good and nice activities seek to distract us from those Key Result Areas. Wise people refuse to be sidetracked by the nice at the expense of the important.

Saying "no" is not easy. When I am asked to consider an opportunity, my usual answer is "I will think and pray about it and get back to you." Rarely do I agree on the spot. Often I will consult one of my trusted colleagues for a second opinion on whether the opportunity is one that is truly important. After thinking, praying and considering my schedule and Key Result Areas, I will accept or decline. I am learning that saying "no" can be very powerful in accomplishing what God has called me to accomplish. Saying "no" allows me to say "yes" to the key missional things God has called me to do. I cannot say "yes" to those without saying "no" to other good things.

KRAS AND SWEET SPOTS

Intentional living means I am ministering out of my strengths and the Key Result Areas for my work must be in alignment with how God wired me and, therefore, where I can be successful. In Chapter six, we discussed the concept of 'sweet spots,' the importance of knowing what our sweet spot is and ensuring that we are spending 60-80% of our time ministering out of our strengths. This is key to success with our KRAs because God wired us the way He wired us for a purpose, and it is only when we are working in line with our gifting that we will be happy and productive.

A word to those who are just starting out in ministry—you may not yet have clarity on your strengths although the testing we have suggested can help. Time has a way of helping us understand ourselves as we try different things, so pay attention to areas where you are strong and where you are not and you will start to discern your strengths.

We indicated that trying to make weaknesses into strengths is not a good strategy because it just won't happen. How do we deal with areas of weakness? One of the reasons for team is that with differing gifts there is a good chance someone on your team is strong where you are weak, so look around for someone who can pick up what you are not good at. I have a 'support system' for areas of weakness where I know I'm no good and need others to help. If there is nobody, go find somebody! Or, consider the option to just stop doing what you are not good at. Sometimes that is the best option—as long as it is not a critical part of your role.

If in reading this and the prior discussion on sweet spots you feel that you are totally out of your area of strength, don't ignore that. Trying to do a job that is not within an area of strength will be deeply frustrating, and your frustration will spill over to others, and you will not be the productive person God made you to be. Be intentional in finding a job that is better suited to you.

HI leaders have a significant responsibility to ensure that those who report to them are ministering out of their strengths. To do otherwise is to set up people to fail and to compromise our mission.

ANNUAL MINISTRY PLANS

Key Result Areas do not necessarily change from year to year unless the focus of one's job changes. KRAs are the broad definition of success. What does change is the Annual Ministry Plan (AMP), which describes *how* one is going to fulfill each of the Key Result Areas in a given year.

HI Definition:

Annual Ministry Plans (AMPs) are the specific steps one is going to take in any given year to fulfill one's KRAs.

Before the beginning of a year (whether a calendar year or a ministry year), all members of a team should have determined both their KRAs as well as the specific plan they intend to drive to fulfill those KRAs. These plans are developed by the individuals who must drive them and are then endorsed by their supervisor. They are specific enough to be measurable and form the basis of the monthly coaching/mentoring meeting with the supervisor.

Annual ministry plans ensure good planning

At the heart of intentionality is a commitment to thoughtfully and prayerfully think through what needs to be done and how one should do it. It is the difference between accidental and intentional living. This may be a stretch for people who are not used to planning, but they will get used to it and the results of their work will be measurably better.

Intentionality is about understanding what the end goal is (KRAs) and how one should best get there (AMPs). While the secular world has long stressed such planning, the ministry world has been significantly behind, especially when it comes to focusing on results. Good ministry is impossible without good planning.

Annual ministry plans help everyone measure progress

Another advantage of AMPs is that supervisors and team members now have a way to measure progress. There is a plan and monthly mentoring/coaching meetings can use this plan to gauge progress. Because the team member developed the plan him or herself (with supervisor sign off), they can be held accountable for its execution.

For individuals, the Annual Ministry Plan provides the roadmap for the year in terms of what they need to concentrate on. The hard part is done (knowing what to do) and now one can concentrate on executing the plan. This is a wonderfully helpful tool for self management. It puts the responsibility for ministry execution on individual team members rather than on the team leader. It empowers and provides for accountability.

There are people in the ministry world who believe that results do not really matter. I am told on occasion that "the only thing that matters is faithfulness." While faithfulness is a nonnegotiable, results do matter because they matter to God. We are all about much fruit (John 15). Annual Ministry Plans help us measure how much progress we are making according to the plans we have laid out.

Annual ministry plans form the basis for annual reviews

The ministry world is notoriously lax in helping people know the success of their performance on an annual basis. With KRAs and AMPs, it is possible to have an objective annual performance review. How did the team member do in fulfilling their AMP and therefore fulfilling their KRAs? Even if not done perfectly (perfection is not the goal, intentionality is), the presence of an identifiable plan makes evaluation objective and easier and forms the basis of the next year's Annual Ministry Plan.

KRAs and AMPs provide for both empowerment and accountability

In the absence of KRAs or AMPs it is difficult for a manager not to control or micromanage. After all, they don't know what their team members might be doing. In order to empower, one has to clearly define the expectation, which is done through

KRAs and AMPs. Then on a monthly basis, there can be a mentoring/coaching check-up that is driven by the Annual Ministry Plan.

CONNECTING THE COMPASS TO THE CLOCK

The world is filled with good intentions. And that is all that Key Result Areas and Annual Ministry Plans are unless they are intentionally connected to how we use our time. If KRAs and AMPs are our compass, our schedule is our clock. Once we have defined success, the most critical element in living intentionally is to actually connect our intentions with our schedules.

Apart from Scripture there is no document more important to us than our schedules. The one asset that we cannot get back is our time. How we spend our time (activity) has a direct impact on the results of our life and work (success). HI Teams do not live by the seat of their pants, or on the fly. Many people do, but High Impact people do not. And HI leaders do not allow their team members to live that way either. They don't settle for accidental living.

It has been said that one can tell a lot about a person's priorities by their checkbook. The same can be said for schedules. I often ask my senior leaders to share their schedule with me. I can tell from looking at their schedule what their true priorities are. My own schedule is available to all my key leaders. They can look any time they choose. It is my way of setting an example of how I connect the compass to the clock and it makes me accountable to those I hold accountable. I cannot ask of others what I do not practice myself.

Schedule your priorities

Our priorities are our Key Result Areas, and the Annual Ministry Plans are the annual roadmap for achieving our KRAs. Either we schedule time in our month to work on our AMPs or life and others will schedule us instead. Either we control our time or others will control our time.

A simple way to do this is to schedule your week with blocks of time carved out for your priorities. Blocks of time allow you to focus your attention on specific issues which are in line with your Annual Ministry Plan. Once you have scheduled your priorities you can fill in the rest of the schedule with the meetings, administration and other activities that are a part of your life.

I color code my schedule so that I can track where I am spending my time and determine at a glance whether I am giving adequate time to the five KRAs I have.

As you schedule your priorities, think about the time of day that you will be most productive for a specific task. I do much better in the morning with focused blocks of time (this morning I started writing at 4 a.m.). Afternoons (for me) are better spent in meetings, answering email and taking care of administrative tasks.

Do not allow administrative duties to take precedence over those activities that will drive your AMPs and KRAs. Even senior leaders can be fooled into thinking that they are using their time strategically when in reality they are not. Unless our time use can be directly connected to accomplishing our mission and accomplishing our KRAs, we are confusing activity with results.

Control your interruptions

Focused individuals develop tools to control interruptions to scheduled time. There are blocks of time when the phone should not be answered and when email should not be read, when we are not accessible to others except in the case of emergencies. Most of us are good at keeping appointments that we have with other people. My approach is that an appointment on my calendar for focused work is as sacred as an appointment with a person. And I work hard to keep both of them.

We know that life interrupts, so leaving margin in one's schedule allows flexibility *when one must adjust*, which should happen more seldom than not. Remember, either we control our schedules or others will do it for us. We make the choice as to how intentional and disciplined we will be with the most important asset we have—our time.

Schedule thinking, reading and planning time

A secret of HI individuals is that they set aside time in their schedule to think, read and plan. They put into their schedule specific days or even weeks during the year when they will be out of the office, away from distractions with time to let their minds connect the dots in ways that they never would have if they had not taken the time.

When we give our minds the opportunity, we will connect dots about our lives and ministries that can revolutionize our effectiveness, strategy or paradigms. The key is that we give our minds the opportunity. Schedule it in!

If you are a visual person, use a whiteboard or journal to jot down ideas or sketch out diagrams. With time, these thoughts will marinate until you come to clarity. Effective people take the time to think—intentionally.

Don't do what others can do

There are things that only you can do in your role. There are many things that others can do as well or better than you. Be ruthless in delegating to others those things that you do not need to do. This allows you to focus on what you must do and on those priorities you have determined by KRAs and AMPs.

Every year I ask the question, "What things can I give away to others so that I can focus more directly on the most important things I must do?" This allows me to 'up my game' and be more effective as a leader.

HI Best Practice:

Think through your schedule and make a list of all the activities that someone else could do rather than you. If it is not critical for you to do and if someone else can do it 70% as well as you, give it away. By doing so you have a chance to 'up your game,' which is the name of the game.

Build in accountability for schedules

Because connecting the compass to the clock is so critical, I strongly suggest that team members be asked to show their team leader their schedule during their monthly mentoring/coaching meeting (chapter eight). This is not to control, but to build in accountability for how we spend our time and to give the leader opportunity to coach and probe as to how the team member could be more focused and strategic in time management.

If your team is using common scheduling software, make the sharing of calendars a standard practice and ask team members to be specific about what is on the calendars. There is great peer accountability when there is clarity around how people use their time. Leaders set the pace by their own discipline and being transparent about what they are up to. Trust is generated when others know what you are doing.

HI Best Practice:

Make all calendars available to supervisors, peers and team members.

Identify your top three priorities each month

None of us can concentrate on everything. On a monthly basis, identify the top three priorities that you are going to concentrate on. These should be directly connected to your KRAs and AMPs. These priorities should be reported to one's supervisor along with a report on the results from the top three priorities of the previous month.

Foster a culture of execution and results

Execution, the discipline of getting things done, is a focus of HI Teams. It is not about activity but about results. As teams meet, or as supervisors have their monthly coaching/mentoring meeting, the discussion should always include results, not simply activity. By focusing on real results that are in alignment with the organization's mission and team members' KRAs, we send a strong message that it is not about activity but results. Many ministries do not have a culture of results.

When one reads the New Testament there is a major focus on results. Think of the many admonitions of Paul regarding how we live our lives so that we run the race well and are worthy of the prize. The book of Acts stresses the fruit (results) of the growth of the early church including the number of people who were added to the church. Jesus emphasized the results of changed lives in those who claimed to follow Him. He said that if we stayed connected with the vine we would see much fruit (results) in our lives. Paul's mission to Ephesus (Acts 19), resulted in the whole region being influenced with the gospel (results).

Remember, our lives are not about activity but about God-honoring results of that activity. Because we are missional in our thinking we are always seeking the best-possible results of our activity. Foster that kind of culture and your organization will be better for it.

PERSONAL RETREAT DAYS

A large part of helping your team be successful is to ensure that they stay in alignment with their Key Result Areas and their Annual Ministry Plans. This is facilitated by a monthly Personal Retreat Day (PRD) spent outside of the office for planning and evaluating one's life and work against the KRAs and AMPs they have adopted for the year. Personal retreat days follow the example of Christ who regularly went off by Himself to spend time with the Father in prayer and meditation.

The purpose of the Personal Retreat Day is not to take a day off. Rather it is to:
- Review KRAs and AMPs
- Make necessary adjustments where one is out of alignment
- Determine the top three priorities for the coming month
- Review the top three priorities of the prior month
- Spend time thinking and praying about upcoming obligations. This includes thinking through possible

engagements that you have not decided on in light of your priorities spelled out in your KRAs.

- Spend time in prayer asking for wisdom and guidance
- Perhaps spend time in a key personal or work-related book
- Write your monthly prayer update to your personal prayer team

Often, when I teach on intentional living people will respond to the PRD concept with "I don't have time to do that." My response is, "You don't have time not to do that," because intentionality is the key to productivity, not endless activity. The more carefully we think through the priorities of our lives the more productive we will be. What is needed is usually not harder work but smarter, wiser work. It is amazing what happens when we take the time to stop and think and pray. It is perhaps the most important work we do because it is the key to effective work.

HI Definition:

Personal Retreat Day: One day each month, planned on the calendar and set aside for planning, thinking, prayer, review of KRAs and AMPs, and writing a monthly prayer letter. It is usually off site, without other appointments or interruptions.

With our KRAs and AMPs, we have a roadmap for our year. We may have to adjust to circumstances but we can self manage for maximum results rather than settling for activity and hoping for results. In addition, because our supervisor has endorsed our KRAs and AMPs, there is no need for him or her to 'manage' us, nor do we need to manage those who report to us, other than to ensure that they stay focused on their KRAs and AMPs.

Key Result Areas and Annual Ministry Plans foster a culture of empowerment because once the KRAs are defined, each team member has a great amount of freedom to determine their Annual Ministry Plan and the strategy they will employ to meet their KRAs. Leaders and supervisors become encouragers, coaches, consultants and equippers rather than primarily managers and directors.

People are trusted to figure out how to accomplish their annual goals in a culture of empowerment with accountability. Good people thrive on empowerment and accountability in an environment of clear expectations and maximum trust. This is the environment that KRAs and AMPs help to build in a great organization.

PERSONAL PRAYER TEAMS

Some years ago, a dear friend gave me the greatest gift anyone could give. He volunteered to set up a personal prayer team for me and my family. He brought together a number of couples from around the country who loved us, were committed to us and whom we trusted. This formed the inner core of a prayer team that has sustained us over many years.

This inner, core prayer team is one with whom we feel free to share anything that is going on in our lives—whether marriage, family, work or other issues. We communicate with them at least monthly, sometimes more. They are committed to complete confidentiality and we are committed to being transparent with them. They have sustained us through many dark days and many bright ones.

We also have a second, larger prayer team of several hundred people who are committed to praying for us. I typically send out a short report of the past month, my calendar for the current month, as well as any special requests we have as a family. I am convinced that any success I see in my job is a direct result of the prayers of these dear partners. How grateful I am that they have faithfully upheld me, our ministry, my wife and her ministry, and our two boys.

HI ministry is not possible without regular intercession by ourselves and by others who pray regularly for us. As Paul indicated, we are involved in a spiritual battle that requires spiritual weapons (Galatians 6). The more intercession we have, the more protection we have. I for one want all the protection and power I can appropriate.

Because the Personal Retreat Day is a day of evaluation, planning, alignment and prayer, it is a great time to update one's prayer team for the coming month. Not only are we touching base with our priorities and plans, but we are touching base with our Lord and those who uphold us before the throne.

HI Best Practice:

Develop two prayer groups to uphold you, your family and your ministry. An inner, core group with whom you can be completely transparent regarding issues you are facing. This requires a commitment on their part to be confidential and your part to be transparent. Then develop a larger, outer core group who can pray for you on a regular basis. Your commitment is to keep them updated monthly on those issues for which you would like prayer.

ANNUAL PLANNING RETREATS

If planning is the key to intentionality, then an annual planning retreat for all key ministry personnel must be part of their job and rhythm. I recommend at least a three-day retreat for thinking, planning, prayer and finalization of the next year's Annual Ministry Plan. As I indicated previously, Key Result Areas will often not change unless the focus of one's job has changed. However, the Annual Ministry Plan will change each year since last year's plan was accomplished and the coming year builds on the previous year.

Following this planning retreat, two additional steps are necessary. First, a meeting with one's supervisor to review the AMP and ensure that the supervisor is in agreement since this will become the basis of the monthly meeting and annual review. Second, it is helpful for each member of the team to share their Annual Ministry Plans with the others to ensure that there is alignment between the plans and efforts of all members on the team.

If your team is working off of 'team KRAs,' it is important to define those team KRAs before individuals develop their own KRAs or AMP, since the individual KRAs and AMP must support those of the team.

NEVER NEGLECT THE SOURCE

Proverbs 4:21 says, *"Above all else, guard your heart, for it is the wellspring of life."* As Christ followers who are involved in His Kingdom work, this is the single most foundational principle for living intentionally. We choose to intentionally guard our hearts because the passions, contents, desire and purity of our hearts influences all of our decisions, priorities and Kingdom impact. What we do with our hearts influences everything about who we are and where we are able to lead others. We cannot lead others where we have not gone!

Choosing to be intentional and proactive in growing our relationship with Christ is the single most important decision we can make. Intentional means that it is regular, not haphazard; planned into our schedules, not an afterthought; a priority, not ancillary. Realizing that we connect with God and grow in different ways, my goal is not to prescribe *how* you do this but to challenge you to give it a high priority. I practice what I call 'unhurried time with God' on a regular basis where I have the time to pray, listen and meditate.

There are three reasons why this time with Christ is so critical. The first is that, according to Jesus, our lives are simply an overflow of our hearts (Matthew 7:15-20). Think on that for a moment. The more we immerse ourselves in Christ, the more our lives will simply overflow with content that is His. It is an unconscious result of living in His presence. One cannot manufacture this, it is either there or it is not and it comes from guarding our hearts.

Second, as people who are in ministry we need wisdom and insight into strategies, people, situations and problems. Who has the insight that we need? The closer we are to Christ, the more 'audibles' we will hear where God literally drops ideas, information or answers into our hearts and we say "That's it!" All of us have probably had that happen. God is heard most easily by listening ears and open hearts and those senses are tuned by spending time with Him.

Third, we are in the business of leading others closer to Him. We can only lead people where we have already gone. The closer we stay to Him, the better we can lead people to Him.

HI Moment:

How well are you doing in guarding your heart? Would you say very well, average or marginal? Do you have an intentional and proactive plan to stay close to Christ that makes this a high priority in your schedule? Do you need to revisit this area of life so that you are more intentional?

HI Moment:

- On a scale of 1 to 10 with 10 being deeply intentional, where would you place yourself on the intentionality scale?

- What is the hardest discipline for you in regard to intentionality?

- How do you see the connection between God-given opportunity, life call and intentionality?

- Is there currently a good connection between your top priorities and your sweet spot? Explain.

- What things do you do that you could have others do?

- Do you find it easy or difficult to say "no" to expectations that do not fit your priorities? Why?

SAMPLE KRAS AND AMP FOR AN ORGANIZATIONAL LEADER

KRA One: Personal Development

Summary: Ensure that I live intentionally in my spiritual, family and professional life.

Goal: Stay on track with Jesus

Plan: Daily unhurried time with Christ, read through the Scriptures, practice a monthly retreat day, keep a journal and communicate with prayer teams monthly.

Goal: Stay focused

Plan: Monthly retreat day, annual retreat, prioritize schedule according to KRAs and delegation of issues that can be delegated.

Goal: Keep marriage vital

Plan: Weekly date with Mary Ann when home, pray regularly together, keep her current with my work, and travel together when possible.

Goal: Be engaged as a dad

Plan: Find ways to connect with Jon and Steven, pray regularly for them and always be available to them.

Goal: Grow my leadership quotient

Plan: Read and think regularly on leadership and missions, develop relationships with other mission leaders and continue to write for the church, leaders and staff.

Goal: Be accountable

Plan: Invite accountability and input from a key group of friends, from the ReachGlobal board and be transparent with staff on schedules and priorities. Keep my prayer team aware of needs and schedule.

KRA Two: Strategic Leadership

Summary: Provide strategic leadership to ReachGlobal (RG) values, mission and vision for the future, and through annual strategic initiatives.

- Review and finalize all current key documents of RG to ensure a common voice and proper alignment
- Drive intentional diversity in RG domestically and internationally
- Help RG move toward greater multiplication in all of our ministries
- Champion the ReachGlobal Sandbox
- Provide maximum clarity to the leadership and personnel
- Ensure the smooth launch of LIVE[0]
- Provide regular communication to personnel re: vision, opportunity, and strategy
- Work with the chair of the ReachGlobal Board to ensure the board contributes the greatest value possible to ReachGlobal strategy
- Realign schedule for less activity and more 'think time'
- Ensure benchmarking of new metrics
- Develop relationships with national movement leaders
- Complete a book on 'Missions in the Color World' by June 2009

KRA Three: Strong Team

Summary: Build a strong, unified, aligned, strategic and results-oriented team to lead ReachGlobal.

- Design March and November meetings that are venues for networking, training, encouraging and missional alignment
- Spend time with Directional Leaders to encourage, coach and be aware of their ministry world and needs
- Model the leadership qualities and commitments that we have articulated for all leaders in ReachGlobal
- Ensure that all RG personnel are trained in the concepts of 'Leading from the Sandbox' over the next 24 months

KRA Four: Leadership Development

Summary: Develop current and future leaders of ReachGlobal and influence national partners.

- Ensure the intentional development of the Lead Team through annual events, clusters and communication
- Ensure the completion of the Leadership Pipeline with job descriptions, competencies and training necessary for each level and ensure the training of leaders consistent with the Pipeline
- Ensure that leaders are mentor coaches, that ReachGlobal personnel receive monthly coaching/mentoring from supervisors and that all individuals and teams are using KRAs and AMPs
- Intentional personal mentoring of 10 individuals at various levels in the EFCA to develop the next generation of leaders
- Ensure that leaders are identifying and mentoring potential leaders in ReachGlobal regardless of the level in which they currently work

KRA Five: Mobilize Resources

Summary: Mobilize key resources necessary for ReachGlobal to flourish and build for the future.

- Keep prayer initiatives in front of leaders and staff
- Ensure that GVP hits its financial goal this year and raise new resources for the International Leadership fund and other strategic projects for RG
- Identify and challenge leaders within and outside of our EFCA movement to consider joining ReachGlobal in leadership roles
- Ensure regular communication with missions pastors and mission committee members via a broadcast email and Sandcastles

SAMPLE KRAS AND AMP FOR A TEAM MEMBER

Big Rocks for this year:
1. Coordinate and launch new EFCA Web site
2. Transition to/acquire new responsibilities
3. Focus on multiplication in admin processes/procedures

KRA One: Personal Development

Summary: Focus on holistic health and growth including spiritual, relational and physical health.

1. Grow in spiritual health and in my relationship with God
   a. Take monthly personal retreat day
   b. Take on one new responsibility at church
   c. Memorize two 10-verse sections of the Bible
   d. Read one book on faith
   e. Spend time in the Word at least once a week for 20+ minutes
   f. Pray daily for marriage, family and work

2. Grow in relational health
   a. Spend intentional quality time with my husband alone each week
   b. Spend intentional quality time with my son each day
   c. Talk with my sisters at least 2-3 times per week
   d. Talk with my family members once per week
   e. Spend time with one other couple at least once per week

3. Focus on optimal physical health
   a. Get at least 7 hours of sleep / day
   b. Spend 30+ minutes, at least 3 days/week in an aerobic work out
   c. Limit to 2 sodas/coffees per week—always decaf
   d. Train for a triathlon

KRA Two: Strategic Leadership

Summary: Give strategic leadership to administrative support staff and strategic ReachGlobal initiatives.

1. Align administrative support staff with mission/vision of EFCA ReachGlobal

   a. Monthly team meetings—inform team of leadership decisions, initiatives, etc.

   b. Review Sandbox once a year

   c. Develop KRAs for admin team

   d. Meet monthly with direct reports

   e. Assess administrative processes to ensure multiplication

2. Lead ReachGlobal staff through new strategic initiatives

   a. New Web site—launch in October

   • Work with ministry leaders to assess their needs for the new Web site

   • Elicit and coordinate up-to-date content for the new Web site

   • Be the primary communicator to ReachGlobal staff regarding new Web site

   • Coordinate with and activate the divisions within Reach Global to develop strategic approaches to using the new Web site AND train others to manage/filter the information posted

   b. Communication developments/publications

   • Be primary communicator to ReachGlobal staff regarding communication publications

   • Work with admin staff in their execution of communication publications

   • Assess ReachGlobal communication needs and work with Director of Communication to create solutions to those needs

KRA Three: Strong Team

Summary: Focus on building a team that is unified, motivated and proactive in supporting the mission of the EFCA and ReachGlobal.

1. Meet with admin staff team regularly

  a. Monthly team meeting

  b. Monthly coaching/mentoring meeting with direct reports

  c. Affirm behavior that is proactive, positive, motivated and missional

  d. Help team function as a network that understands other team members' work and responsibilities

2. Focus on team building and community

  Admin staff

  - At least one admin team retreat day annually

  - Do a team building exercise quarterly during our monthly meetings

3. Focus on transition

  a. Train/mentor another individual to take on and succeed in my role and responsibilities as admin team leader

  b. Pursue additional challenges and responsibilities in team leader roles

KRA Four: Staff/Individual Development

Summary: Focus on effectively developing staff and individuals both within and outside of ReachGlobal.

1. Ongoing training

  Facilitate and advocate ongoing training for administrative support staff

  - Project training

  - New Web site training

  - Skills-based training opportunities (job specific)

2. Meet with admin staff regularly

    a. Monthly mentoring meetings with staff

- Continue to help facilitate goals for them to achieve for development in their job
- Ensure their processes support multiplication

    b. Monthly team meetings

- Advocate ongoing training
- Host trainings for the teams to experience together
- Ask questions about what skills/training they need to do their jobs more effectively. Follow through with proper training opportunities.

3. Develop myself as a leader

    a. Attend at least one conference that provides leadership training

    b. Pursue additional leadership responsibilities in and/or outside of ReachGlobal

    c. Meet with leadership mentors once per month

KRA Five: Mobilizing Resources

Summary: Assist in acquiring and wisely distributing resources for maximum ministry effectiveness in ReachGlobal.

1. Administrate and oversee EFCA EQUIP sites for the following teams:

    a. ReachGlobal Board site

    b. ReachGlobal Directional Team site

    c. ReachGlobal Lead Team site

    d. ReachGlobal Internal site

2. Oversee ReachGlobal publications

    a. Oversee content of ReachGlobal publications and sub missions

    b. Ensure that information is readily available to Reach Global staff, as well as EFCA staff

    c. Ensure content is mission-critical to the ministry of the respective audience

3. Mobilize materials that support the ministry of our personnel

    a. Update personnel regularly with available resources. Respond to requests for material within 24 hours of the request.

    b. Assess what materials are necessary for the ministry of our personnel to be effective and assist in providing solutions or suggestions on how to accomplish those solutions

4. Mobilize information and resources to assist Executive Director of ReachGlobal

    a. Respond to ED's request for info within 24 hours of his contact

    b. Anticipate information and resource needs before they arise and communicate those to the ED

    c. Write any necessary drafts or documents on behalf of ED

    d. Participate in all ReachGlobal Directional Team Meetings and disseminate necessary information throughout the organization

CHAPTER EIGHT
Becoming a Mentor/Coach

Good team members do not want to be 'managed' or controlled, but 'released' to become the best they can be.

Great leaders desire the same for their team and take an intentional posture of a mentor/coach.

Coaches love to release the gifting and potential in others by making meaningful time for the people who report to them. They probe, ask questions and help their people think well and come to healthy conclusions. They care about the whole person, help them find their 'sweet spot' for maximum joy and effectiveness, and hold them with an open hand. They want the very best for those they coach.

Mentors give honest and direct feedback to their reports so that their people are clear on areas where their performance is great and where it is problematic. They practice a 'no surprises' policy and provide help when issues of performance or EQ are sub-standard.

Mentor/coaches use carefully crafted monthly meetings to ensure that their people stay on track—in line with their KRAs and AMPs. This allows good people to flourish and eliminates the need for micromanagement. Annual evaluations have no surprises as honest feedback takes place on a monthly basis.

Good leaders use the mentor/coach paradigm to build great teams, develop their people and keep them aligned. They make the tough calls when necessary to remove unproductive people so the mission is never compromised.

Great leaders love to develop great people and they make it a priority!

What does it mean to be a supervisor? For many the word 'manager' comes to mind. But think about that. Do you like to be 'managed'? For many, that word spells control and is not a cool or empowering word. What it says is that my manager does not trust me to do the job I have been hired to do or that two people need to have a hand in doing my job—my manager and me.

One of the most frustrating issues good people face is the sense that they have too little freedom to use their gifting, skills and creativity to accomplish the work they have been hired to do. Controlling supervisors seldom develop HI Teams because the best people will not sign on, or if they do sign in, they don't stay on.

Do you really want to 'manage' others? Most ministry leaders and supervisors I know find the traditional job of 'managing' others frustrating and time consuming. And it should be because good people were not made to be managed. They were made to be empowered, set free and then coached and mentored. If people on your team cannot be set free, empowered and then coached, you have the wrong people on your team.

The whole point of intentional living with KRAs, AMPs, and PRDs is to unleash and empower good people while maintaining maximum alignment and accountability within the ministry. These provide a roadmap for good people to follow that, with the agreement of their supervisor, gives them the skills to manage themselves and their work.

This changes the equation for everyone who supervises others. With good people (right people, right seat) who are living intentionally (with KRAs and AMPs) and are in their sweet spot (their responsibilities match their gifts), you no longer need to manage. Your job changes from managing and supervising to coaching and mentoring. Which would you prefer? Your people know which they prefer.

I am going to make a distinction between mentoring and coaching. They are different sides of the same coin, each with its own focuses. A good team leader needs to practice both, depending on the circumstance.

THE PRACTICES OF COACHES

One of the great privileges I have is to be the coach of a number of people. Having passed the 50 mark, my real work is to unleash other great people who will be the next generation of leaders in our organization and in the church. So I make a personal commitment to formally or informally coach 10 individuals at any time.

A coach has a certain mindset of releasing gifting and potential in others. It is the mindset that I have every time I meet with someone to whom I am a coach. Some of these are people who report to me, others are simply those in whom I see great potential.

Coaches want to release the gifting and potential in others

Coaching is not about helping others become like us! Or having them do things the way we would do them. The world does not need another one of us. Coaching is about releasing the gifting and potential in others and helping them become as successful and impactful as they possibly can be.

'Release' is a key word for a coach. Good people have been gifted by God with unique skills and particular ways of approaching problems and situations. Coaches want to tap this potential and these gifts, pulling them out so that the gifting and potential are released in increasingly productive and effective ways.

Leaders who think that life is all about them will never make good coaches (nor do they deserve to have good people working for them). Coaching is one of the most selfless things we can do because our focus is on helping others be successful and allowing them to get the credit. The most loved and effective leaders are those who take this selfless approach toward those they lead. When our people know that we are committed to making them successful they become the most loyal team members we have.

This is consistent with what we have already noted—leaders must lead through their team. The more successful their team members are, the more effective the leader is. Leading is all about releasing the potential in others. That is what coaches do.

Coaches don't tell, they ask

Releasing the potential in others means that our challenge is not to tell people how we would do things if it were us, but to help those we coach figure out how to solve problems and meet challenges themselves. Coaches ask questions, lots of questions, questions that make others think and come to good conclusions. This is a challenge for many leaders who are ready to tell others what to do or how to proceed. On occasion this is necessary. Releasing others, however, means that we are committed to helping them decide how to proceed. Telling them does not do that.

One of my most-trusted colleagues, Gary, is the best I have ever seen at asking questions. Sometimes I have to say, "Enough already!" When you meet with him he probes, questions, circles back to ask a different way, always trying to clarify and help you think. He is not necessarily trying to help you come to his conclusion but to a good solution. Through his questions he helps people understand motives, gifting, options, potential solutions, and ways to achieve maximum impact.

Because coaching is interactive, we need to take the time necessary to dialogue. For people who live on the fly this will mean a change in how we approach people. On-the-fly people have no option but to tell people what to do because they don't have time for anything else. But this approach disempowers others if practiced consistently. Caring about others and their development means that we are willing and committed to take time with them whether face-to-face, by phone, or as often happens in our global organization, by using communications software.

Coaches care about the whole person

Many leaders and organizations simply use people. Such organizations don't make the annual 'best places to work' list. While good organizations, teams and leaders are deeply missional, coaches understand that there are many factors in a person's life that affect their work, their emotional health, and their makeup. Caring about the whole person is one of the keys to unlocking potential.

There are a constellation of issues that should be explored on a monthly basis with those you lead. One of the questions I frequently ask those in our organization is "What is your happiness factor?" (one to ten). When I ask the question I am not specifying that it is only job-related. I want to know how the individual is doing—generally. If I get less than a seven I will ask the follow-up question, "What is going on?" and most often, people are very frank in their response. If it is job-related, whether or not I can do anything about it, at least I know there is an issue. If it is a personal issue, I can at least pray. And the individual knows that I care—about them (not just their work).

If it is job-related, I will often ask, "What would make your happiness factor greater?" Sometimes I will find out that they are feeling boxed in, or that a supervisor is not empowering them or that they are bored and need a greater challenge. The question allows me to follow up and see if we can solve the issue. But again, they know that I care—and when I follow up they really know I care.

Coaches are exegetes of those they coach

People are different and need to be approached differently. People cannot be treated alike in a cookie-cutter way. Individuals are just that—individuals, and our approach, whether mentoring or coaching, needs to fit who they are and the wiring they have.

I have had great people on a variety of teams. One of them would periodically come into my office and need to talk—maybe for 45 minutes or so. He wanted me to know what was happening in his area. Sometimes he sought counsel but really it was 'connection' time. Once done, he worked in a highly productive manner but the connection time was crucial.

Another team member likes to pop in two-to-three times a week—sit down, debrief, and then pops out again. She will give me crucial information she thinks I need to hear and then leave it with me.

My assistant is someone who needs 'context' for issues. If she fully understands the context, she is highly productive. I know that when I ask her to work with me on an issue, that giving her the context will help her do what she needs to do.

Our organization does a fair amount of testing to help people understand their wiring. That testing also helps supervisors know how to work with, coach, and mentor them in a way that is consistent with their wiring. In fact, I want my team members to understand my wiring as well. The better we understand one another the better we work together, find synergies, avoid conflict and encourage each other. People are not the same and we should not treat them the same.

Coaches hold people with an open hand

The ultimate test of whether we want the best for those who work with us and for us is: Do we hold them with an open hand? Are we willing to develop them for their sake even if it means that we end up developing them out of the organization?

Holding people with an open hand and wanting the best for them engenders huge loyalty and appreciation. The message we give is that we ultimately care about them, and what God wants for their lives, not what we want for their lives or what we can get out of them. When we try to control others we are violating them and may be violating God's best for them.

People do not belong to us, they belong to God. Our commitment ought to be to help them be the most effective they can be, become everything they can become and use their gifts to the maximum. If this is our commitment, people will know and appreciate our care. If it is not our commitment, people will know and resent our attempt to control.

I tell those who report to me on my senior team that I hold them with an open hand, will always seek the best for them, will help them develop and thrive, and will never stand in their way should God lead them elsewhere (even though it would not be my choice). I also ask them to trust me and tell me if they are thinking of leaving so that we can at least talk. If there is something that I can do to change something that would keep them engaged with us, I want the opportunity to do that. If they are clearly being led elsewhere I want to help them in their transition. Of course I cannot mandate this, but because they believe that I want the best for them, in almost every instance this has happened.

Coaches always try to keep their people engaged

People, especially highly motivated people, are not static. They grow, they change, they get bored, and they periodically need new challenges. My philosophy is that I want to find the very best people I can find and then keep them highly motivated by changing their responsibilities when I need to.

One is better off being flexible with job responsibilities and therefore keeping great people than to see them go because the organization is not flexible enough to flex with them. This is all about playing to people's strengths and keeping good people with the organization where possible. At each annual review I ask the question "If there were things you could change about your job what would they be?" With good people, I do my best to reconfigure where I can to keep them as engaged as possible.

THE PRACTICES OF MENTORS

If being a coach is one side of the coin, being a mentor is the other. Mentors are more direct than coaches and there are areas where leaders need to be direct to help those they lead grow and move to their next level of effectiveness. Taken together, the practices of mentors and coaches give you a healthy balance in your supervisory role.

Mentors give honest feedback

Constructive feedback is often missing in ministry organizations where the culture is supposed to be 'nice.' The lack of honest feedback hurts the individual and the organization. It does no one any favors and can eventually result in people actually being let go for behaviors that might have been modified if someone had been courageous enough to be honest.

Kay is a missionary in Europe (name and location have been changed) who has a strong personality. She comes across as demanding (what she needs from her people, she needs now), arrogant (does not listen to what others have to say), and has a history of short tenure in any one place since no team is good enough for her and consequently no one wants to work with her.

The only way to help her is for a supervisor to be absolutely honest about how her behaviors affect other people (both missionaries and nationals) and that her behaviors are not acceptable in an organization that places a high priority on healthy people and healthy teams. It may be that no one has confronted Kay about such behaviors but a healthy leader will. A mentor will give honest feedback and clarify what behaviors are acceptable within the organization and which are not. And then hold her accountable!

Mentors get people individual training when necessary

Kay, and others like her, needs some intense time with a professional who is trained to help people understand their behaviors and their negative impact on others. Good mentors not only provide honest feedback but also, where necessary, insist that an employee or team member receive help that will allow them to be more effective.

In our organization, this often means help from a psychologist or a good mentor, especially when someone is dealing with behaviors that negatively impact their own lives, the lives of others or those of their team. Our commitment to healthy missionaries and healthy teams makes intervention a necessity when there is significant lack of health. We do it for the sake of the employee, the organization, the team they are on and their long-term effectiveness.

Too often, Christian organizations are not redemptive where they need to be, ignoring issues that should be dealt with, and compounding the problem by eventually letting someone go without ever being honest or finding a way to get them the help they need. This does not honor the employee, the organization or God.

Mentors care about their people
but they also want a winning team

Leaders build teams that can win. Yes, we know it is not about the game; in fact it is about something far more important— God's Kingdom. HI leaders are committed to results, insist that the team play well together, that players are playing to their strengths, and that the results are consistent with the mission of the organization.

This means that if changing the responsibilities of team members to better organize the team for effective ministry is necessary, they will do it. It also means that there are times when they need to let someone go because they cannot play at the level needed in their ministry role, or the person is not effective in their job even after intensive mentoring. Leaders must dismiss people on occasion for the sake of the team—and for the sake of the ministry. We want to be grace-filled and redemptive in the process, but good leaders do not allow the mission of the organization to be compromised by keeping people who are not effective.

The dual practices of intentional living with KRAs, AMPs and PRDs, and leaders who are dedicated mentor/coaches are designed to help team members be effective, fruitful and productive. If, with all of these tools, a team member cannot perform, they need to be transitioned to a place where they will be fruitful (if possible).

Sometimes the organization has outgrown a person's capacity. Sometimes an individual is not in their sweet spot and should no longer be in your organization. Sometimes they are just lazy and unwilling to take the steps necessary to be as productive as you require your team members to be. Sometimes there is an EQ problem that even with mentoring and intervention cannot be overcome (or the individual is unwilling to overcome).

Once you come to the conclusion that things are not going to change and that you need to make a change, do it as quickly as possible—with the best counsel you can get so that you are legally compliant from an HR perspective, and smart since people have constituencies. Be as generous as you need to be so that when people inquire you can justify both the decision you made and the process you followed. But don't ignore the problem. It will only create greater problems if not dealt with wisely and quickly.

THE MENTOR/COACH MONTHLY MEETING

HI leaders avoid two traps that ministry people often fall into. The first is to simply assume that everything is fine and not spend one-on-one time with direct reports because it is a distraction to other things you choose to do. The second is to micro-manage and disempower your reports by not allowing them to develop their areas of ministry. Neither of these two practices will help you develop a results-oriented, aligned and productive team.

A best practice is to schedule a monthly mentor/coach meeting where you can play both the mentor and the coach depending on the circumstance, encourage, provide feedback, remove barriers and ensure that the individual is tracking with their Key Result Areas and Annual Ministry Plan.

Before the meeting

Your scheduled monthly meeting with reports should take place *after* their personal retreat day. During their PRD, they should fill out their monthly report, which provides you the basis for your meeting and discussion. The form we use in our organization is shown below.

Monthly Staff Feedback

Please complete as part of your personal retreat day and forward to your supervisor.

Name: _____ Date: _____

1. My 'happiness factor' this month?:
   (10=High; 1=Low)

2. I need a decision or information from you on the following items:

3. Relationship(s) with the following person/people has 'gone sideways' recently:

4. I'm having a problem with the following roadblock(s):

5. Here are the results of my top three priorities from last month:

6. Here are my top three ministry/work priorities for next month:

7. Currently, my most challenging issue is:

8. Here's how I am doing in the following areas of my life:

    (**10**-Great; **8**-Very Good; **6**-OK; **4**-Slipping; **2**-Not Well; **0**-Awful)

    ___ Spiritually ___ Mentally ___ Emotionally

    ___ Physically ___ Relationally ___ Personal Evangelism

    Further comments I would like to share with you about these areas:

9. You can be praying for me and/or my team regarding the following:

Why these questions?

These questions are specifically designed to help supervisors understand where their people are on a monthly basis. Whether or not they are covered in the monthly meeting depends on what is recorded by the team member. A good mentor/coach wants to understand where people are at, what issues they are struggling with, what they need from their supervisor, what they are working on, and the results of their past month's priorities. This short form which can be quickly filled out gives the mentor/coach valuable information about where their people are at.

My 'happiness factor' this month (10=High; 1=Low)

As explained earlier, the point of this question is to find out where people are at in a general way. Their answer will be a combination of various factors in their lives, some professional, some personal, some related to circumstances they are facing. Whatever the number is, the follow-up question is "Why?" What are the issues contributing to the number they gave you? Questions like, "What would make it higher?" or "What are the contributing factors to your number this month?" can help you scope out areas of concern, joy, frustration or motivation that are influencing your team member.

By asking this question on a monthly basis, you are able to get the 'temperature' of your team members and information that can help you understand and coach them more effectively. You also have an early warning system that can help you keep individuals motivated and fulfilled in their jobs rather than finding out one day, to your consternation, that they are un-happy and moving on. This simple question will give you a great deal of information on a regular basis.

I need a decision or information from you on the following items:

It is not unusual for a team member to need a decision or information from their supervisor to move forward. This ques-tion is simply designed to remind or inform the supervisor that something is needed from them before their team member can move forward.

Relationship(s) with the following person/people has 'gone sideways' recently:

Relationships that are not in sync are one of the most common dysfunctions of working relationships, and left alone, they hurt cooperation, trust, effectiveness and integration. This question is designed to help your reports keep short accounts and quick-ly deal with relational breakdowns, where they occur.

As a mentor/coach, the supervisor has the opportunity to help their team member determine how best to repair bro-ken relationships or deal with conflicts that have occurred. It also sends a powerful message to team members that your organization (and you as their leader) is committed to healthy relationships and the principles of Matthew 18.

I'm having a problem with the following roadblock(s):

Roadblocks are issues that need to be resolved before your team members can move forward, but which they cannot resolve by themselves. They may need the cooperation of another individual or department that they are not getting. It could be a funding issue, a decision or an organizational barrier that they need someone at a higher level to resolve.

One of the key responsibilities of leaders is to remove barriers for those who report to them. Where there are barriers, commit to a plan with your report as to how you will help remove the barrier, put it on your calendar and carry through as promised.

Here are the results of my top three priorities from last month:
Here are my top three ministry/work priorities for next month:

These two sections go to the heart of intentionality. If someone cannot identify their top three priorities for the coming month, they are not carefully thinking through their coming month on the Personal Retreat Day. These three priorities must tie back to their Key Result Areas and to their Annual Ministry Plans. If the supervisor does not believe the priorities for the coming month are truly strategic or important, this gives an opportunity to dialogue about priorities.

Equally important is requiring a monthly update on the results of last month's priorities. Remember, leaders care about results and asking the question, probing where necessary, and holding direct reports accountable for what they committed to last month sends a strong message that results matter. When there is a pattern of unacceptable or unfulfilled results the leader has concrete and objective means to discuss the issue of performance.

This is a place where you can ask about how your report is doing in their Annual Ministry Plan—a reminder to them on a monthly basis that your expectation is that the plan is being worked and will in large part be fulfilled. Neither you nor they should be surprised at the end of the year regarding the AMP because you have been discussing it on a monthly basis.

Currently, my most challenging issue is:

Again, this is information you need and want to know. The issue may be one you know about; often it will not be since you are not aware of all that goes on in your report's world. Since it is a challenge to them, it gives you an opportunity to be a mentor/coach and ask questions, probe and help them discover ways that they might approach the challenge. Challenges are growth points when handled well so you will want to pay close attention to these areas and how your report is handling them.

Here's how I am doing in the following areas of my life:

*(**10**-Great; **8**-Very Good; **6**-OK; **4**-Slipping; **2**-Not Well; **0**-Awful)*

___ *Spiritually*   ___ *Mentally*   ___ *Emotionally*

___ *Physically*   ___ *Relationally*   ___ *Personal Evangelism*

Further comments I would like to share with you about these areas:

We are not one-dimensional people and the essence of the mentor/coach relationship is that we care about the whole person. Even asking the question on a monthly basis means that your report must think about the important areas of her or his life and determine a grade. It is a reminder that health in all aspects of life matters—and influences their lives at work. It also tells them that you care about them as a person, not simply for what you as an employer can get out of them.

Low scores in any of the areas can spark a healthy conversation about what they are doing or could do to bring their score up. Asking good and probing questions is the most effective way of getting at issues.

Maximizing the monthly coach/mentor meeting

A commitment that HI leaders make to those they lead is that they will set aside quality time on a monthly basis to meet with them. In the best-case scenario this is a face-to-face meeting, but in global organizations it will often be by phone or using technology like Skype or Net Meeting. The key for supervisors is that they are fully engaged, mentally and emotionally, during this time—giving the best that they have as mentor/coach to those they supervise.

While you have asked for and received a structured monthly report, I suggest that you do not rigidly follow a specific outline but vary it so that the discussion does not degenerate into a boring or routine dialogue.

Start by getting a feel for what is happening in your report's life. The small talk matters because it reinforces relationship and because the issues in our lives are impacted by the stuff of life, good and bad. You also want to know your team member as well as you can, so even the small details matter.

While you may talk through specific issues that they have already reported to you in the monthly report, you should have some well-thought-out questions that will allow you to probe in areas where you believe your team member needs growth. I actually make a list of the issues and questions that I want to talk about prior to the meeting so that my contribution as a mentor/coach is as productive as it can be. I also think through the approach that I will take in areas where my report might react defensively. I want to get at issues without causing defensiveness or raising unnecessary walls where possible. I am there to help them, not hurt them and unless their behavior or work requires significant improvement—and therefore direct feedback—I will seek to get at issues without raising defenses. Wherever possible I will use questions to get at issues that I want to address.

When direct feedback is required, I will be direct in saying something like, "Let me give you feedback on how you reacted in our meeting," or, "I'm going to coach you on this issue." In the case of significant performance issues it pays to be very direct. People who are performing well require mentor/coaches. People who are not performing well, need very direct feedback with clearly defined expectations for performance improvements.

When there are performance issues, *always* make a written record of your conversation and send a copy to your report of the issues you discussed and the action steps you require. Not only are you making your evaluation and expectations clear, you are also keeping a paper trail in the event that you need to let them go. In that case, you want a clear record of the issues you had and the process you used to rectify the situation before termination. Keep those records in a secure place in the event that legal action is threatened or taken against the organization.

While good people are granted great latitude in their work (empowerment with accountability), the strategy with problematic people is to keep shrinking their box and clarifying your expectations until either their performance improves, they decide to leave because of the pain, or you have the evidence of continued poor performance that you need to let them go.

HI Best Practice:

Keep expanding the box of empowerment of good team members and keep contracting the box of empowerment of problematic team members until their performance improves, they self select out, or you have what you need to let them go. People who perform well deserve expanded freedom. Those who don't perform well deserve diminished freedom.

As you walk through the monthly mentor/coach meeting, keep notes on key issues that you discuss so that you can review them prior to your next meeting. In addition, keep an electronic or hard copy of the monthly report form for future review.

ANNUAL PERFORMANCE REVIEWS

In the absence of Key Result Areas and Annual Ministry Plans, annual reviews are a frustrating experience for supervisors and reports. The frustration comes in quantifying success, having clear expectations and sorting out results from activity. To say the least, it can be a nebulous evaluation around foggy expectations—even with great team members.

Key Result Areas and Annual Ministry Plans change the whole equation. Now there is clarity around what spells success (KRAs) and around what one is being evaluated on (AMPs). There is now an objective basis on which a team member can evaluate their own performance (our goal is to help good people lead themselves) and on which supervisors can evaluate them.

Because of the monthly mentor/coach meeting, there should never be a surprise during an annual evaluation. If there are surprises, it means that the supervisor has not been giving honest feedback along the way and frankly, that is unfair to the report. A team member should have a very good idea as to what their supervisor will say at the annual evaluation because they have been talking about any issues on a monthly basis.

Annual reviews are tied directly to KRAs and AMPs. Thus the first step is for the team member to do a self evaluation around their KRAs and AMP.

HI Best Practice:

Tie annual evaluations not to anniversary dates of team members, but to the close of one ministry year and the start of another. This way, annual reviews are tied directly to the completion of KRAs and AMPs and the start of a new round of both.

A sample Annual Review Form that can be used as the basis for the review is shown below:

Staff Member Annual Review

Name: _____ Date: _____

1. Comments on KRA accomplishments:

2. What is mission critical for this next year and needs to be reflected in next year's KRAs and AMPs?

3. Comments about relational growth this past year:

4. Comments about personal growth this past year:

5. What personal development goals need to be included in next year's KRAs and AMPs?

6. Comments about general work/ministry effectiveness:

7. Recommendations for any necessary growth/ development:

Supervisor's signature: _____

Staff member's signature: _____

Comments on KRA accomplishments:

This is a straightforward process. All one needs to do is to take their KRAs with their AMPs under each KRA and comment on what they have accomplished during the year. What we want team members to have done during the year is 'work the plan.' The percentage of their plan that they have worked is a key indicator of their success for the year.

A perfect score is not necessarily the goal. When people first start to use KRAs and AMPs they are often optimistic as to how much they can accomplish during the year. In addition, life happens and sometimes it is simply not possible to complete the plan. What the supervisor wants to see is intentionality and a high degree of follow through. Those two combined will help people accomplish far more than they probably were previously able to when there was not clarity on success and plan.

What is mission critical for this next year and needs to be reflected in next year's KRAs and AMPs?

The prior year's KRAs and AMP become the basis on which we plan for the next year. Generally, KRAs do not change unless responsibilities have changed. Before you meet for the review, your report should have completed their Annual Planning Retreat, filled out their part of the evaluation, and completed their Annual Ministry Plan for the following year.

Your best people will always be harder on themselves than you will be. Celebrate with them the wins they have experienced in the past year and be clear on how their work has positively contributed to the organization and its mission. Thank them for the part they have played on your team!

The annual review then provides an opportunity not only to look back but to look forward and to dialogue about their identified KRAs and AMP for the coming year. Those KRAs and AMP should logically continue to drive their ministry down the road and build on what has already been accomplished. In other words, there should be a direct connection between one year's plans and the next.

Comments about relational growth this past year:

Competent people continue to grow relationally throughout their lifetime. Given the importance of EQ, leaders should dialogue with reports about areas where growth would be helpful.

Comments about personal growth this past year:

What personal development goals need to be included in next year's KRAs and AMPs?

The personal growth KRA is always the first KRA because it impacts our spiritual, emotional, professional and family lives. For believers, it is core to who we are and who we want to become.

For this reason, dialogue around this question is significant in an annual review. When people get into trouble it is almost inevitable that an area of their personal lives has been neglected. Supervisors owe it to their reports to probe, encourage, ask good questions and help them to be all that they can be in this area of life.

This should naturally lead into the question of what needs to be honed in personal growth in the coming year and whether the AMP reflects the necessary priorities. Because the posture of a mentor/coach is to help their reports be all that they can be, make specific suggestions where you think that development would strategically enhance a team member's work.

Comments about general work/ministry effectiveness:

Because our focus is not on activity but on results, this question goes to the heart of how a team member and supervisor see the overall effectiveness of the individual's work. Are they playing at the level they need to be playing at in their job and on your team? Are they effectively using their time and energies in the most strategic way and concentrating on issues that are truly priorities? Are they finding ways to leverage their work for greater effectiveness? Are they doing multiplication rather than addition? Is their work focused on missional rather than ancillary issues?

One of the questions a supervisor should ask in the midst of this discussion is "What do you need to do next year to go to the next level of effectiveness in your ministry?" Every year, each of us ought to be able to identify several areas where we can take the next step in effectiveness by delegating something to someone else, by reprioritizing our time or by making a few strategic decisions. Helping reports identify these steps for the next year will help them grow in their ministry. These should then be reflected in the report's AMP.

Recommendations for any necessary growth/development:

Because mentor/coaches want the best for their people, they will give careful thought to additional growth and development opportunities that have not already been covered above. We want each team member to grow in significant ways every year.

THE SELF LEADERSHIP OF HI LEADERS

HI leaders can be mentor/coaches of those they lead only if they have the moral authority of their own lives that gives their mentoring, coaching and leadership intrinsic authority. People will follow those whom they respect, who live what they talk and who are out in front of those they lead. Without the moral authority that comes from self leadership, they will only engender cynicism of those they lead.

Self leadership requires us to set the pace for those we lead with a high degree of intentionality and discipline, personal development and growth, living the rhythm of KRAs, AMPs and PRDs, and a commitment to results that is based on well-thought-through priorities. Those we lead know whether we live that way or not. Do not ask of others what you are not willing to model! In fact, as good as the suggestions in this book may be, if you are not willing to take the lead and walk the walk, don't ask your team members to do it.

There is significant pressure on leaders today to stay current and keep growing. We must lead the way in ongoing growth, professional development, personal, emotional, spiritual and missional growth—or move aside and let someone else lead.

The issues that we covered in this chapter apply to leaders first and foremost. Lived out, they become part of our lives and they then naturally overflow into those we lead, mentor and coach. As Jesus said, we are the overflow of our hearts. Leaders are the overflow of their lives. If something is not resident in our lives, it cannot 'flow over' to others. We can fake it for a season, but not for long.

I have made my KRAs and AMPs public to the organization I lead. They have a right to know that their leader lives by the same disciplines that I ask of them. Are you willing to do the same?

WHO ARE YOUR MENTORS?

The higher one is in a ministry organization, the less likely one is to be intentionally coached and mentored by someone else in the organization. Indeed, you may be the leader of your organization, so who coaches you? Who holds you accountable for intentionality and results? Hopefully you have a board that does some of that, but boards may or may not know what you are doing (it is more likely in a local church where boards meet more often).

HI leaders make themselves accountable by bringing around them other leaders who consistently ask good questions, even when the questions are uncomfortable ones. They develop a constellation of mentors (no one mentor can meet all of our needs) whom they meet with to intentionally learn from and grow. They read selectively to learn from others. And they discipline their own lives so they can lead by example first, and by teaching second.

I can count about 10 mentors in my life. They include the senior team I serve on as we sharpen one another, my co-leader in the organization I lead, a brother, a father, two close friends whom I regularly see and a handful of others. In addition, I intentionally cultivate friendships with people whom I believe that I can learn from and contribute to. Almost everything I practice I have learned from others. The moment I think I am self sufficient is when it is over for me as a leader.

If I were to slip from the life I espouse, there are people around me who will gently but honestly confront me. Who are those people for you?

HI Moment:

Take a moment and list the mentors in your life:

_____

_____

_____

_____

360 DEGREE ANNUAL EVALUATIONS

A best practice for leaders is to have those who report to them contribute to their annual evaluation in some kind of 360 degree feedback process. We may think we are modeling what we espouse—what do those who work for us think? How about asking? There is nothing like honest feedback from teams to help leaders know how they are doing and where they can grow.

This takes an attitude of 'nothing to prove and nothing to lose,' and a real desire on the part of the team leader to accept constructive feedback and continue to grow in their leadership.

HI Moment for Leaders:

- How does the mentor/coach paradigm described in this chapter compare to your approach? What changes do you need to make?
- What style of management do you personally prefer? Why?
- How good are you at providing honest feedback to your reports?
- Who are your mentors? What do they provide for you?

HI Moment for Team Members:

- What style of management do you prefer? Why?
- Which mentor/coach practices described in this chapter would help you do a better job in your role?
- Who are your mentors beside your supervisor? What do they provide for you?

CHAPTER NINE
Dangerous Transitions

Organizational leadership transitions are dangerous moments, regardless of the level at which they take place.

Transitional moments must be handled with great care if they are to succeed. This includes understanding the leadership pipeline within the organization—the various levels of leadership that exist and the specific sets of competencies and values that characterize each level.

Not everyone is wired to be a leader. To place someone in leadership of others who is not wired to be a leader is to hurt them and those they lead. Remember too, that everyone has a capacity beyond which they will not be successful. Thus, the process of leadership selection is critical.

In order for these transitions to succeed, it is crucial that transitioning leaders are closely mentored and actively coached throughout the process. Part of this transition is helping them give up the values and requirements of the prior level and take on the values and requirements of the new level. They are not the same.

Most organizations do a substandard job of identifying and training a leadership 'bench.' Some organizations are not even friendly to leaders. Good leaders are always identifying potential leaders and have a process in place to groom them for the next leadership level.

Negotiating transitional moments for success is a high priority of good leaders and healthy organizations.

Why do some people who transition from one level of leadership to another (either within one organization or moving from another organization) succeed while others fail? Many transitions from one level of leadership to a higher level are painful—both for the leader and for those they lead. There are few moments that are more dangerous for leaders and organizations than these transitions. If they fail, they hurt people on the team and damage the confidence and ability of the one who was making the transition.

A TRUE STORY

Dave was a successful recruiter for a ministry organization. Year after year he excelled at recruiting personnel for short-term teams and led a team of other recruiters, most of them just out of college. Dave was liked by his team, was a great recruiter, could communicate well, was mission driven and had a good reputation in his organization.

Because of his skills, Dave caught the attention of a Christian placement organization and when a senior position in another Christian organization (a denominational office) came along, he was convinced to put his name in the hat.

The denominational office was looking for someone who would serve at a senior team level and lead a team of highly qualified professionals in several divisions. They interviewed a number of candidates with a long list of credentials, but none of the candidates fully fit the culture and ethos of the denomination, or they operated in paradigms that were not consistent with the leadership model of the denomination, or they simply were not qualified.

When Dave's resume came in, it looked impressive. Several interviews with leaders of the denomination went exceedingly well. Dave had done his homework and knew what to ask. He was confident and articulate and all the references strongly supported Dave for the position.

Dave was subsequently hired with great anticipation of his success. Quickly, however, warning signs appeared. He would spend a great deal of time in his office with his door closed leaving staff members wondering what he was up to. When he met with staff members, he listened to very little and didn't ask them questions about their areas of responsibility. In senior staff meetings, he often seemed to be in his own world and was not engaged in issues the team was dealing with. Furthermore, his supervisor found that there were serious gaps between his own understanding of what Dave was responsible for and how Dave saw his job.

Dave's team was patient, but one by one they expressed doubts to their prior supervisor about Dave's fit for the leadership role. Team meetings were skipped and cancelled. What had been a cohesive team started to fragment with each member doing their own thing. Their previous camaraderie was gone. Dave's supervisor continued to spend time with him and assumed that the pain was simply a result of a leadership transition.

He was wrong. After a year of substandard results that were chalked up to figuring out the new job, Dave's supervisor started to confront the issues more directly. As the supervisor started more intentional coaching, Dave withdrew into his world more and more. Eighteen months after his hire, Dave resigned and went back to a recruiting role.

What went wrong here? The denomination had used a qualified search firm, procedural due diligence had been followed, references had been checked, coaching and appropriate supervision had taken place and Dave was a person of character who had a history of success. Dave's success as a team leader had been strong in his previous position, but in this one it was not. In spite of his confidence and skills, he had not been able to fulfill his job responsibilities and had continued to withdraw. It was a leadership transition that did not work and the pain was paid by Dave, his team, his supervisor and the organization. All felt like they had somehow failed in the process.

UNDERSTAND THE RAMIFICATIONS OF TRANSITIONAL MOMENTS

Leadership transitions are dangerous moments whatever the level at which they take place. When they go well, everyone is happy. When they go wrong, the organization suffers and sometimes, good people choose to leave because they feel they have been dealt a bad deck with a dysfunctional or unqualified leader.

In analyzing this transition, the supervisor went back to look at the level that Dave had played at in his prior organization and realized that he had led a lower, mid-level team of young people. At the denominational office, he was leading a team of proven professionals at a senior level. In addition, while Dave saw himself as a great team leader, his understanding of team was a group of people who spent a lot of time together with lots of social interaction. At the new job, the team was a missional team, not a fellowship team, and Dave frankly did not know how to lead a missional team. In addition, he was intimidated with the professionalism of those he led.

Dave had been promoted above his level of competency at this season in his life and as a result was over his head, did not know how to lead at that level, and was subsequently positioned to fail. His failure was not a reflection of his character in any way or of his basic competency. It was a reflection that he had missed some key leadership transitions that he should have had before he led at the level at which he was expected to lead.

One of my colleagues, Daryl Anderson has done an extensive study of leadership transitions within our organization. Notice the top 10 answers to two important questions regarding these transitions:

When you have observed someone who did not transition well from one leadership position to the next, what were the reasons? What did you observe?

1. Lack of adequate preparation, training and orientation to the new position

2. Wrong assumptions and expectations about fit and needs for the new ministry

3. Could not switch from doing ministry to leading others to do ministry

4. Lack of EQ/people skills

5. Lack of gifts for the position

6. Could not switch out of their former role into a new role with a new set of needed competencies and priorities

7. Did not understand the organizational changes from one level to the next

8. Were not able to manage a larger ministry

9. Could not switch between self motivation and instruction to motivating and instructing others

10. Promoted because of longevity in the mission rather than gifting for the new position

When you have observed someone that did transition well from one level of leadership to the next, what were the reasons the transitions went well? What did you observe?

1. Active coaching throughout the transition

2. Good preparation for the transition

3. Strong sense of call that was affirmed by others

4. Adequate knowledge of the ministry they would be leading

5. Good communication skills

6. Displayed real concern for the people they were leading

7. Possessed healthy EQ

8. Clear that they were gifted for the role—in their sweet spot

9. Exhibited a servant heart—leadership was not about them but others

10. Learned the job well and approached it with a learning spirit

What is clear is that transitional moments must be handled with great care if they are to succeed. And the stakes are high because if the transition fails, there are impacts to everyone who works for the new or promoted leader. Issues like EQ, job fit, understanding of the role, knowing how to lead and coach others, servant leadership, communication skills, ability to gain the respect of those they lead, organizational understanding and proper leadership maturity for the new role are all crucial. Given the complexity, it is no wonder so many transitions run into trouble.

Our organization was forced to look carefully at how we made these transitions because historically, the mission had not highly valued leadership positions, had not proactively trained leaders before they were placed into leadership roles, and had fostered an administrative role for leaders rather than a strong leadership role. Often there was no evaluation of true leadership ability. Instead, people were placed into leadership roles because they were the only willing individuals, had shown success at something else they had done or were popular with their peers.

The net results were mixed. Where leadership ability was low, those reporting to them felt significant frustration. Where it was high, it was more about God's mercy than good planning. On selection to my role as the senior leader of the mission, the first issues I was confronted with were areas where non-leaders were in leadership roles causing angst, frustration and conflict for both the leader (who was not gifted for the position) and those they led. My consulting experience tells me we are not the only organization that has paid too little attention to whom we put into leadership roles and how we train them for those roles. In this regard, ministries are far behind the secular world.

One of the unhealthy cultural realities of ministry organizations (this is especially true of mission organizations but it infects others as well) is that personnel see themselves as 'independent contractors' who essentially are hired to do their own thing. Denominations see this mentality when various levels do not work with each other. Churches see this in siloed ministries that pay no attention to the rest of the ministry. Mission organizations see this when missionaries see their sending organization as simply a nice way of getting to the field, but with no corresponding responsibility back to it.

The thesis of this book, of course, is that this kind of thinking will never make for HI Teams or HI ministry. Issues of leadership, alignment, missional focus, intentional plans and integrated efforts are all critical to making the greatest ministry impact. Who we place in leadership and how we prepare them for their roles all become an important piece in this puzzle.

UNDERSTANDING LEADERSHIP PIPELINES

A great deal of study has been done about what is called the leadership pipeline[6]. The thesis is that every organization has specific levels of leadership that need to be understood and taken into account when making leadership transitions. For instance, in our mission organization there would be six distinct levels of leadership:

1. Self Leader: This applies to all of our personnel. Intentional living for personal and ministry development.

2. Ministry Leader: Leads a particular ministry on a team.

3. Team Leader: Spends 50% of time leading others on his/her team. Has completed team-leader training.

4. Area Leader: Full-time leader who leads other ministry team leaders and is responsible for the management of an area. Reports to an International Leader and has completed area-leadership training.

5. International Leader: Reports to Executive Director, has broad area of ReachGlobal (RG) responsibility, including leader, ministry and organizational development and leads one of the four RG divisions.

6. The Executive Director of the Mission: Responsible for all RG ministries, is the leader of RG senior team, serves on the EFCA senior team, and answers to the EFCA President.

Similar levels of leadership can be identified for those who serve in the National Office of the mission and support those who work globally. The rule of the leadership pipeline is that one should never promote someone from one level to another without insisting that they go through each level in between. In other words, we would not promote someone from level two to level five. Rather, we would insist that they go through levels three and four first.

Why? Because every level of leadership requires a specific set of competencies and values. Moving from one level of leadership to the next is always a transition.

---

[6] For an excellent discussion on leadership pipelines, see Ram Charan, Stephen Drotter, and James Noel, *The Leadership Pipeline: How to build the Leadership—Powered Company,* (San Francisco, CA: Jossey-Bass, 2001)

When Joel, discussed in an earlier chapter, had difficulty flying at 30,000 feet and wanted to dip down to 5,000 feet to do things he had previously done, he was having trouble making the transition from one level to another. If one allows someone to skip a level of leadership, they miss something very important in the process, and because they have never experienced that level of leadership, they are missing some critical information that they need to have.

That is also the struggle that Dave the recruiter had. He had missed at least two turns in the pipeline, leaving him without the core competencies to lead a team at the level that was required. Neither Dave, the search firm that was used, or the denomination that hired him recognized that he was not ready for the level of leadership he was being hired for. And, having skipped several turns in the pipeline, he was destined to struggle and ultimately fail in the new position.

It is not important that the individual has gone through all levels of the pipeline in your organization. It is not unusual for us to bring someone into ReachGlobal from the marketplace. What we want to know in that case is that they have gone through similar levels and that they have not skipped any crucial turns.

Different pipeline turns require different competencies and skills

The role of an independent producer (someone who basically works by themselves and does hands-on work) is very different from a team leader who must lead through others. That in turn is very different from someone who supervises multiple team leaders (such as an executive pastor in a large church). The differences are significant. At each level, there are different competencies needed, different job descriptions, different scopes of vision, and a different way of thinking about life. Unless your organization understands the different competencies and the differing roles at each bend in the leadership pipeline, you run significant risk of a difficult or failed transition.

To illustrate, I will use the example of a large church and the various staff members on the team.

Support staff member: The job primarily provides administrative support. There is not a great deal of decision making involved but good judgment is required along with competence in needed areas and the ability to work on a team with others. The focus is primarily on one's own work. One could also put the typical ministry volunteer in this slot. Flies at 5,000 feet.

Support staff leader: The job provides administrative support and gives leadership to other staff members. Requirements include the ability to mentor and coach others; build a strong, unified, results-oriented team; organize effectively for the best results; and manage conflict. The focus is on managing one's own work and ensuring that the team is doing well, and that direct reports are managing their work well. These competencies and focus apply to volunteer ministry team leaders as well. Flies at 10,000 feet.

Pastor/administrator: The job leads a particular ministry or support area. Requirements include being a self starter, knowing how to self manage through KRAs and AMPs, using time efficiently, working with others in a staff team, possessing high EQ, communicating and working well with others, being responsible for their area of work and probably deploying and leading a team of volunteers. Focus is missional, primarily on what one is personally responsible for but is also aligned with other ministries with some focus on volunteers who are part of the specific ministry or administrative area. Span of control and responsibility is significant but focused on one's own ministry. Flies at 15,000 feet.

Supervisor of pastors or administrators: The job leads a team of professionals focused on a specific area of ministry such as youth or children. Requirements include being a self starter, knowing how to self manage through KRAs and AMPs, empowering others, using time efficiently, leading through others, building a strong, unified, aligned, results-oriented team, possessing high EQ, communicating and working well with others, being responsible for results of the team's work, and being a mentor/coach. Focus is missional and primarily on others to ensure the success of the team. Span of control and responsibility are significantly larger than in level three requiring the ability to think more globally. Flies at 20,000 feet.

Executive pastor: Same as that of a supervisor of pastors or administrators with the additional requirement that they are able to think globally, take into account the whole ministry of the church, be excellent team builders, and keep everyone focused on the mission, values, central ministry focus and ethos of the church with a focus on results. In addition, they must be able to negotiate multiple constituencies including the staff, the board and the senior pastor whom they serve. Their fingerprints are on everything but their name is on nothing. They are quintessential servant leaders who keep the ministry in alignment, people working together and they 'lead from the second chair.' This requires a high level of EQ, the ability to lead from behind the scenes and a humble servant leadership style. Flies at 30,000 feet.

Senior pastor: The senior pastor is the senior leader of the organization with three primary focuses: preaching the Word (either himself but more likely leading a teaching team); developing the mission and vision of the church and guarding its values and ethos; and developing, empowering and releasing key leaders. He is the senior mentor/coach, the one looking at the ministry horizon, is deeply missional, thinks globally and assembles the highest-quality leadership team. He is the keeper of the vision and the senior motivator for missional results. He must possess a high EQ, a humble spirit, know himself well and be comfortable with who he is. Flies at 40,000 feet.

HI Moment:

Take some time as a team or individual and think through the different responsibilities and competencies required at each level in this church pipeline. Identify the differences between each of the six levels.

Can you identify the five or six leadership pipeline levels in your organization?

1_____

2_____

3_____

4_____

5_____

6_____

Be able to identify the pipeline levels in your organization, the competencies needed at each level and the training required for each level of leadership

Once you know what leadership pipeline levels you have, you can determine the competencies needed for each level and the training that is imperative for someone to succeed at that level. A rule of thumb is that the higher the level in the pipeline, the more training and mentor/coaching you will want to do.

ReachGlobal has identified a common curriculum that is required at each level of our pipeline. This gives us a common vocabulary, common training, common skill development and common reading for each leadership level in a global organization. This also makes it possible to transfer a leader to another position at the same level somewhere else in the world and to be training potential leaders to go to the next leadership level in the pipeline.

In addition, at the top two senior leadership levels, all Reach-Global leaders must go through a testing process that measures their capacity, leadership style, wiring, supervisory style and passions to ensure that they are a good fit for the job. Often, such testing confirms what we already think. Sometimes, the testing indicates that the leader is wired to fly at a lower altitude than the new position would require (they will do better with more hands-on work). We will never knowingly place someone in a leadership position at any level that we do not believe they are capable of fulfilling.

Be willing to say NO to potential or current leaders who are not ready or qualified for additional leadership

One of the hardest things for leaders is to be discerning about people they love and respect and to honor the wiring and qualifications they have to lead.

There are three rules that must be honored in this regard. One: not everyone is wired to lead. To place someone in leadership of others who is not wired to lead is to hurt them and those they lead.

Two: everyone has a capacity ceiling beyond which they will not be successful. What we want to do is to grow people to the highest level we can but once they hit that capacity ceiling, honor it or you dishonor them and those they lead. Capacity ceilings come in different shapes and sizes. It may be the ability to think globally, or to fly at the level required, or the span of responsibility needed, or the level of strategy and planning necessary, or the level of mentor/coaching called for. If you promote someone beyond their capacity ceiling, you have set them up to fail.

Three: never make a hiring or promotion decision by yourself. It is simply too dangerous. All of us have blind spots, or we can be enamored by how someone interviews and presents themselves. In our organization if a leader is going to promote someone, they must secure permission from the next two levels of leadership. Why? Because we take leadership seriously and want to ensure that due diligence has been done, that the leadership pipeline has not been violated and that the leader is totally in sync with the mission, guiding principles, central ministry focus and culture of the organization. If there are any red flags, the person doesn't get promoted at that time.

As indicated earlier, we also take testing seriously, particularly at the top two critical levels of leadership. If our testing does not verify our thinking we will not move forward. We also use the services of a job placement professional who conducts the testing and helps us interpret the results. He does not tell us what we ought to do, but we want to know his or her opinion on the fit between the job and the potential leader.

These three rules help us resist the temptation to do the easy thing in cases where we really need a leader (never settle for less than you need), or the nice thing when we really want to please someone who wants the job and whom we like. Both temptations are real. Both are dangerous.

Ensure that leaders are actively mentored and coached during transitions

Leadership transitions are rarely easy, even for good leaders. We should not expect them to be since they are moving to the next level of leadership—territory in which they have not previously operated. In most cases, they will have made transitions in the past so they at least know that there is major change coming.

In these transitions, it is critical that your transitioning leader understands:

- How the new job differs from the old job
- What he/she must give up
- What he/she must do that is new
- How their focus needs to change
- That they will find the transition difficult because there are things they used to do that they really liked doing and shouldn't be doing any more
- What the organization's expectations are at the new level of leadership
- What reading or training you will require of them
- How you will mentor and coach them in the process
- That you will do 360 degree reviews so you know the perception of those they lead and will help them grow in their new role

If there is any period of intense mentoring and coaching, this is the time. If the transition goes south, you have lost significant ground and may well lose a good leader and team members they led. If it is a positive experience, your leadership system gains credibility and your ministry grows.

Leaders always look for leaders to develop

The higher the level of leadership in your pipeline, the harder it is to find competent and qualified leaders. There are two reasons for this. First, even good leaders have built-in capacity ceilings; the higher the level the fewer leaders there are. Second, in many of our organizations we do a substandard job of identifying and training a leadership bench—something that industry and business spend a great deal of time, money and energy doing.

Be on the lookout for leaders at every level of your organization and when you find them, start dialoguing with them about how they are wired and what their passions are. I have found that many who are wired to lead in ministry organizations have not been challenged and are bored in their current roles. Be willing to do some testing if necessary to see if the leadership wiring is there. Then connect them to a mentor/coach (who may or may not be their supervisor) who can help them grow in their leadership abilities.

Ask whether your organization is leader friendly

Many organizations are not friendly to leaders. By this I mean that they do not empower leaders to lead, but are controlling organizations. This is true of many mission organizations. Good leaders will often select out of churches or ministry organizational search processes if they sense that there is not an empowered culture. They want empowerment and they can smell its absence a mile away.

I have noticed in the missions world that there is a higher preponderance of leaders who select fields that are 'creative access' (fields not open to traditional missionaries demanding a great deal of creativity in ministry approach) rather than traditional fields. Why? Because when they look at the traditional fields, they see control, lack of creativity, lack of empowerment and a controlling ethos. When they look at the creative-access contexts they say what the warlords in China used to say out in the hinterlands, "It's a long way to Beijing," meaning Beijing does not know what they are doing! Organizations that are empowered, healthy, and allow for innovation and creativity will see far more leaders surface than those that are not.

HI Moment:

Take a moment and candidly assess how leader-friendly your organization is. If not very friendly, what is needed to change the culture toward its leaders?

Develop current leaders all the time

Your organization will only be as good, as healthy and as effective as the leaders you have, because good people only thrive under good leadership. Thus, the more you pour into leadership development, the better you will be.

This will not happen unless the organization as a whole sees leadership development as a top priority and requires all leaders to be developing other leaders (remember the priorities of a leader). There must be a built-in, organization-wide system that facilitates leadership development or it will not happen. By making this one of the Key Result Areas of leaders, we ensure that it happens. In addition, by developing the training curriculum for each turn in the leadership pipeline, you are requiring every leader to be trained at their level and many for the next level. When you are gone from the scene, your legacy will be the leadership you leave behind.

HI Moment:

- Think through leadership transitions you have been a part of or have watched. When they went well, what were the keys to success? When they were rocky, what contributed to the difficulty?

- Do you have an intentional coaching plan to ensure that transitions within your ministry are positioned for success?

- What are you and your leadership doing to build a bench of future leaders?

- Have you identified the pipeline levels in your ministry, the competencies needed at each level and the training required for each level of leadership?

POSTSCRIPT

Is the building of a strong team simply a nice pursuit or is it a necessary pursuit for long term missional impact? That question was answered for me as I was finishing the manuscript of this book.

On December 4, 2007 I woke up almost unable to breathe. My wife, Mary Ann, took me to the emergency room in United Hospital in St. Paul which turned into a forty two day hospital stay which humanly I should not have survived (you can read the details at www.reachtj.blogspot.com).

Immediately, I was sent to the Intensive Care Unit where I would stay for thirty-two days with massive pneumonia. Within a week I had only 30% of my lung capacity available for breathing as the other 70% was filled with fluid but they could not diagnose the cause and the antibiotics they were using were not working to stem the slide into a critical life-threatening situation.

Because my breathing was so difficult and the pain so severe they decided to put me into a drug-induced coma, intubate me, and put me on a ventilator as they tried to determine the cause of the pneumonia. After a full week in ICU the doctors were able to discover the cause—a highly dreaded and difficult to treat MRSA pneumonia, (Methicillin-resistant Staphylococcus aureus). They started to treat it with a cocktail of antibiotics that they hoped would work fast enough for me to survive.

It was not to be easy. I had already developed pleural effusion (fluid in the lining of the lungs) and some 800ccs were drained from the lining of my lungs and the chest wall. Simultaneously, congestive heart failure set in since my heart could not keep up with the fluid build-up. At the same time, fluid continued to build in my lungs (pulmonary edema) which led to respiratory failure and 14 days on a ventilator.

The consequence of these complications led to ARDS (acute respiratory distress syndrome), which is a severe inflammatory process in the lungs where one starts to drown in their own fluids. Septic shock set in (infection that takes over the whole body) and there was not an adequate blood supply to my major organs. If that was not enough, the mitral valve in my heart failed which led to my heart not being able to pump properly (usually a fatal situation unless repaired by immediate open heart surgery—which I would not have survived).

The stresses on my heart caused atrial fibrillation where my heart tried to compensate for the congestive heart failure, mitral valve regurgitation, and septic shock. My heart was beating at 240 beats per minute and two chest shocks failed to bring the heart rate down.

Just to keep life interesting I also developed encephalopathy (brain inflammation) from the physiological assault on my body and for a while the medical staff were concerned about brain damage.

It would be 42 days in the hospital, 32 of them in Intensive Care, and six weeks after my discharge before I could go back to work—and then only part time. Even as I write this, my energy level is about 60% of what it previously was. In the process of this unexpected chapter in my life, I learned how valuable team was.

It was just a few days after being admitted that the leaders of our personal prayer team flew into Saint Paul to intercede for me. My son Jon informed our larger prayer team of several hundred people and quickly put up a blog that could only be accessed by knowing its address. In the first week, 400 computers accessed the blog and over the course of the next month some 11,000 unique users had joined the concerted prayer for my life. Blog hits came from 75 countries and all fifty states.

There is no question in my mind that it was the concerted prayer of so many and the grace of God that was responsible for my healing. Having a personal prayer team caused a firestorm of prayer as those friends asked other friends to pray and the team grew exponentially and quickly.

I was out of commission for a full three months and after that was able to go back to work on a greatly reduced schedule. During that time, absolutely nothing changed in our organization or ministry even though the things I typically did had to be covered by others. The work was able to continue because of the strong teams that I work with. The senior team of the EFCA picked up responsibilities I had at the denominational level and the senior team of the international mission picked up responsibilities I had there. In fact, things went so well that when I returned I chose not to pick up some of the responsibilities I used to have. I did not need to.

Although I am the senior leader of ReachGlobal, I have chosen to share senior leadership responsibilities with my wonderful colleague Gary Hunter. Not only does he deeply share the mission, guiding principles, central ministry focus and health commitments of the sandbox, but he knows what I know. While we do different things, and play to our strengths, the fact that I had another senior leader so intimately involved in leadership meant that he could pick up my responsibilities without the organization missing a heartbeat—and he did.

When team is done well, it means that there is redundancy in the organization, that no one person is indispensable, and that the culture has been so ingrained in the team that even if the leader were to leave, the culture would remain.

This will not matter to those who think that the ministry or leadership is all about them. It will mean a great deal to those who deeply care about the ministry they are a part of and are seeking to build a ministry that will last. Great leaders and teams are not only concerned about today but are building in a way that the ministry will remain healthy tomorrow—to the extent of their ability to influence the future.

By God's grace (and the intercession of our prayer team) I survived my close brush with death and came back to work with an even greater commitment to ensuring that the team I lead is deep and healthy—and to help other ministries do the same. I realized in a new way how much team matters. Thus, I leave you with these final questions:

- Leaders: if you were taken out of the picture tomorrow, what would happen with your responsibilities and the direction you have set for your team?
- Team members and leaders: is there someone who knows your responsibilities so intimately that they could carry your weight if you were suddenly gone?
- Are you intentionally building for the future health of your ministry rather than simply for today?

If you would like to interact on any of the concepts in this book or share some of your own experience in working with teams, please write me at tj@addingtonconsulting.com. Comments, criticisms and suggestions are welcomed and appreciated.